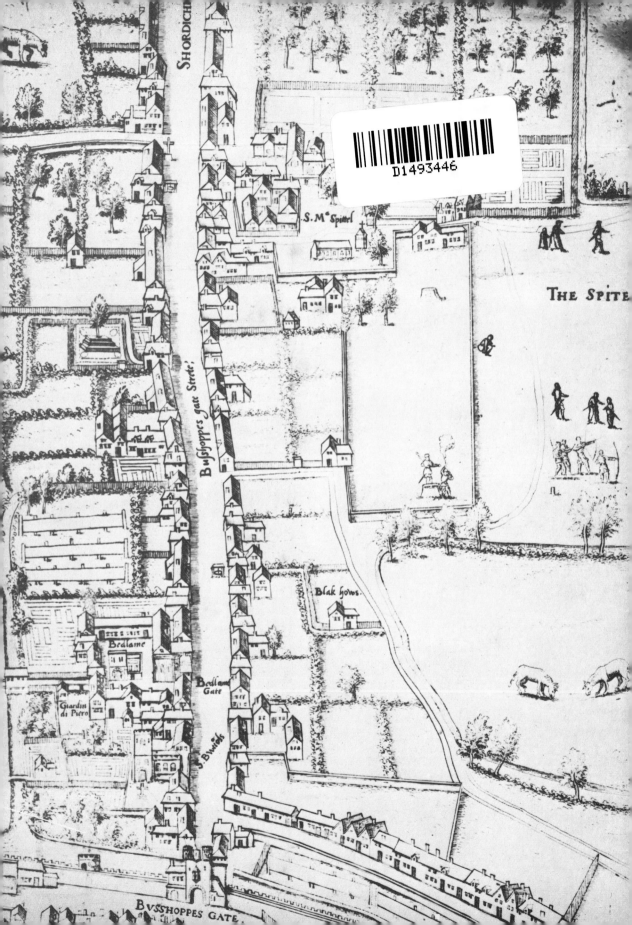

SHORDICH

S. M^s Spittel

THE SPITE

Bufshoppes gate Strete;

Blak hows

Bedlame

Giardin di Piero

Bedlam Gate

S. Butolf

BVSSHOPPES GATE.

The Life and Times of
MARY TUDOR

The Life and Times of
MARY TUDOR

Jasper Ridley

Introduction by Antonia Fraser

VIVAT REGINA MARIA

DIEV ET MON DROYT

Book Club Associates, London

To my Mother

Series designed by Paul Watkins
Layout by Sasha Rowntree

Filmset by Keyspools Limited, Golborne, Lancashire
Printed in Great Britain by
C. Tinling & Co. Ltd, London and Prescot

Contents

Introduction

THE LIFE STORY OF Queen Mary Tudor – 'Bloody Mary' as she has too often been dismissed with contumely – is one of the most poignant chapters in the history of English monarchy. As a child Mary saw her mother cruelly discarded by her father, Henry VIII, for being barren, with her own right to the succession set aside. As a woman, it was Mary's fate to marry a man whom she loved but did not love her: as a wife, she could not bear children despite all her frantic hopes and prayers. Above all, as a queen, she failed to achieve the goal on which she had set her heart – the return of her subjects to allegiance to Rome.

In order to understand the special pressures of an age of faith, it is necessary for us to make an act of imagination to conjure up the particular and complex personality of this unhappy Queen. Mary was never weak, inheriting pride and obstinacy both from her Spanish mother to whom she was intensely loyal, and from her father who she resembled in more ways than is often realised. She had both strength and energy; it was significant that during her feud with Anne Boleyn, Henry's new queen vowed 'that one day she would pull down this high spirit'. Yet despite her bold Tudor promise, Mary was in no sense fitted for the role of a queen, lacking in wordly wisdom as much as political judgment.

One cannot help being fascinated by the mixture of sexual naivety and passion evident in the private life of this daughter of Henry VIII. Jasper Ridley suggests that she had an aversion from sex – reinforced by her father's excesses. Perhaps this would have for ever debarred her from a satisfactory relationship with a husband; certainly she stood little chance with the absentee King Philip II of Spain, who was highly unpopular with the English people to boot. In affairs of state, too, she lived in a world of unreality, steadfastly pursuing her disastrous policy of trying to convert her heretic subjects by force. Her record is indeed unenviable: although she was by no means the only Tudor sovereign to persecute her subjects for religious reasons, Jasper Ridley points out that whereas Henry VII burned ten heretics in 24 years, Henry VIII 81 in 38 years, and Elizabeth 5 in 44 years, Mary burned no less than 283 in a reign lasting only 5 years. So this unfortunate woman dissipated the almost universal popularity which she had enjoyed at her accession, united her subjects in their hatred of Rome, and blackened her own reputation before posterity.

Jasper Ridley, whose previous works include a life of Cranmer, a victim of Mary's persecution, has written a sensitive and revealing account of this, the first female sovereign to reign in England since Matilda. In view of the glorious light with which the age of Elizabeth was shortly to shine forth, it is particularly interesting to note that Mary's rule was regarded as an example of the sort of failure which a woman on the throne was always bound to produce. Indeed Mary's memory has always been overshadowed by that of her great successor, Elizabeth. But in the last analysis justice should be done to Mary too: Mary, the so-called bigoted Catholic, died in the full knowledge that she would be succeeded by her Protestant half-sister Elizabeth. This was an age of political murder, execution and elimination. Nevertheless, in the end Mary preferred the interests of her dynasty to those of her religion. She died, a true Tudor, to be followed by the truest of them all.

Antonia Fraser

Acknowledgments

The author would like to thank Lord Dormer and Mr Farr, the Warwickshire County Archivist, for their assistance with his research.

Photographs and illustrations are supplied by, or reproduced by kind permission of the following. The pictures on pages *15, 63,* 143 are reproduced by gracious permission of HM the Queen; on page 154 by kind permission of the Archbishop of Canterbury; on page *2* by kind permission of the Duke of Bedford; on page 89 by kind permission of Lord Sackville; on pages *50-1* by kind permission of Mrs M.E.Dent-Brocklehurst; on pages *190, 191* by courtesy of Westminster Cathedral Library. Ashmolean Museum, Oxford: 42-3; B.T.Batsford: 108; Bayerische Staatsbibliothek, Munchen: 75; British Museum: *14,* 19/1, 28, 46, 80-1, 83, 84, 88, 98, 100-1, 106-7, 120, 122, 123, 127, 132, 147, 148, 149, 160, 162, 163, 167, 174/1, 174/2, 182/1, 182/2, 183/1, 183/2, 196/1, 196/2, 197, 204-5, 206, 212; Trustees of the Chatsworth Settlement, Devonshire Collection, Chatsworth: 118; City of Norwich Museums: 38; Courtauld Institute: 154; Foto Mas: 19/2, 202; Guildhall Library: 115/1; Landesgalerie, Hanover: 10; London Museum: 28/2, 30, 48, 115/2, 215; Mansell Collection: 87, 90, 95, 111, 164-5, 186-7, 199; Mary Evans: 26, 214; Musée de Picardie: 23; Museo del Prado: 56, 128, 210; National Maritime Museum: 13, 130; National Monuments Record: 104, 104-5, 109, 158; National Portrait Gallery: 16, 17, 35, 61, 62, 73, 76-7, *113,* 155/1, 155/2, 175; Public Record Office: *3,* 24, 153, 168-9, *178, 179;* Radio Times Hulton Picture Library: 52, 53, 74/1, 74/2, 121, 135, 136, 194; Royal College of Surgeons: 66-7; Scala: 37; Society of Antiquaries: *116;* The Master and Fellows of Trinity College, Cambridge: 177; Victoria and Albert Museum: 20/1, 20/2, 28/1, 32-3, 49, 70, *125.*

Picture Research by Colleen Chesterman.

Numbers in Italics refer to colour illustrations.

1
The Young Princess
1516-27

M ARY TUDOR, QUEEN MARY I of England – 'Bloody Mary', as the Protestants in the seventeenth century called her – was born in the palace at Greenwich at 4 a.m. on Monday 18 February 1516. Her father, Henry VIII, was a handsome, vigorous and arrogant young man of twenty-four. Her mother, Catherine of Aragon, was a pious, quiet, intelligent and obstinate woman of thirty.

The Tudor dynasty had not held the throne of England for long. Every Englishman over thirty-five could remember how Mary's grandfather, a rather distant relative of the Lancastrian King Henry VI, had won the crown and made himself King Henry VII by defeating Richard III on Bosworth Field, and ending the reign of the House of York. It had taken Henry VII another twelve years to defeat the revolts of Yorkist Pretenders to the throne, and to convince everyone that, after more than forty years, the Wars of the Roses were really over. Throughout the next century the English people were haunted by the memory of the Wars of the Roses. When foreign visitors to England expressed surprise that the English were so loyal to their Tudor sovereigns, and were prepared to tolerate the despotic governments of Henry VIII, Mary and Elizabeth I, the English told them that they preferred a strong, tyrannical ruler rather than run the risk of another War of the Roses.

In 1501, Henry VII's eldest son, Arthur, Prince of Wales, married Mary's mother, Catherine of Aragon, the daughter of Ferdinand and Isabella, the King and Queen of Spain. Both the bride and bridegroom were aged fifteen. Arthur died within six months of the marriage, leaving his younger brother, Prince Henry, as the heir to the throne; and Henry VII and King Ferdinand agreed that Catherine should marry Prince Henry. By the Canon Law of the Catholic Church, a woman was not permitted to marry her deceased husband's brother; but in the sixteenth century, the Popes often granted dispensations for illegal marriages when great interests of state were concerned, and in 1503 Pope Julius II gave a dispensation which allowed Prince Henry and Catherine to marry.

Although the dispensation had been obtained, the marriage did not take place for six years, because Henry VII raised various political objections; but eventually, in 1509, Henry VII died, and Prince Henry became King as Henry VIII. He brushed aside

PREVIOUS PAGE A young girl playing the lute, painted by the Master of Half-figures. Mary inherited her father's love of music and was taught the lute and spinet.

all the difficulties, and two months after he became King, and
a week before his eighteenth birthday, he married Catherine,
who was aged twenty-three. The new King and Queen seemed
to be very much in love with each other.

Henry VIII and all his subjects were very conscious how
important it was that he and Catherine should produce a son as
soon as possible. In January 1510, seven months after their
marriage, Catherine gave birth to a premature baby. It was a
girl, and was still-born. Eleven months later, on New Year's
Day 1511, a son was born. Henry was delighted, and immediately created the child Prince of Wales; but the public festivities
in honour of his birth had hardly ended before the Prince died
when he was seven weeks old. In 1513 Catherine had another
son, but he died a few days later. Next year she gave birth to a
still-born daughter. Then, towards the end of 1515, the Queen

Een Grave ost Lord
van den Parlemente

Een Lord van
der ordre, zoo sy
ghecleedt
gaen op St
Gooris dach.

Eenen halba
rdier der
Magesteit.

Mary was the only
surviving child of
Henry VIII (far left) and
Catherine of Aragon (left).
Their marriage had been a
very happy one at first but
it became marred by
Catherine's failure to
produce a healthy son.

was pregnant for the fifth time; and on 18 February Mary was
born. Unlike Catherine's other children, she survived.

The birth of Mary Tudor was not celebrated at Court with
the lavish feasts, pageants and tournaments which had been
held when Henry's son was born in 1511, no doubt because it
was assumed that Mary, like all her brothers and sisters, would
not survive. In any case, she was a girl, not a boy, and the
kingdom needed a male heir. When the Venetian Ambassador
called on Henry to congratulate him on the birth of Mary, he
added that the Doge of Venice would have been even happier
if the child had been a boy. Henry replied: 'We are both young;

if it was a daughter this time, by the grace of God the sons will follow.'

Mary was christened at Greenwich two days after she was born, and, as usual in the sixteenth century, she was confirmed immediately after the christening. Henry and Catherine were not present, but most of the lords of the realm were there. The basin was carried by the Earl of Devonshire. Mary was held, while she was being baptised, by two of the three Dukes in England; the Duke of Norfolk held her head, and the Duke of Suffolk, who had married Henry VIII's sister Mary, held her feet. Cardinal Wolsey was her godfather. Her godmothers at the font were the Duchess of Norfolk and Lady Katherine Plantagenet, the daughter of King Edward IV; and at the 'bishopping' (the confirmation) which followed, her godmother was Margaret Pole, Countess of Salisbury, who was the daughter of Edward IV's brother, the Duke of Clarence. One of the gentlemen who held the canopy over Mary during the ceremony was Sir Thomas Boleyn, from Hever in Kent, whose daughter Mary was having a love affair with the King. His younger daughter, Anne Boleyn, was only ten years old, and had not yet come to Court.

Mary grew up to be a healthy child; but Henry needed a son. Two years later, Catherine became pregnant again, and in November 1518 she gave birth to another child. It was a daughter, and died after a few days. Next year, Henry had a love affair with Elizabeth Blount, the daughter of Lord Mountjoy. Elizabeth Blount and Henry had a son, who survived and grew to manhood, taking the name of Henry Fitzroy; but as he was illegitimate, he could not succeed to the throne, and Henry was in the exasperating position that, out of all his seven children, only a legitimate daughter and an illegitimate son had survived.

In the sixteenth century, people were very superstitious, and interpreted all sorts of disasters as signs of divine displeasure. Long periods of drought and bad harvests, floods, unusual thunderstorms, or the stories, which were always being told, of how a calf with two heads had been born in some remote village in England, were seen as proof that some act of policy had angered God. Henry began to fear that his marriage to Catherine was cursed, and that he had sinned in marrying his deceased

18

VERA EFFIGIES
ætatis suæ 52 · 1520

LVDOVICVS VIVES VALENTINVS

brother's wife, even though a dispensation had been obtained from the Pope. When Mary was about six or seven years old, he confided in his confessor that he thought that his marriage to Catherine was not lawful, and that Mary was consequently a bastard. But for the moment he put aside his doubts and continued to treat Catherine as his lawful Queen and Mary as his legitimate daughter and the heiress presumptive to the throne of England.

Like all the other Tudor princes and princesses, and unlike most other girls, even among the nobility, Mary received an excellent education. She was given the best tutors, and studied the works of the leading contemporary scholars, such as Linacre, William Lily, Sir Thomas More, Erasmus of Rotterdam, and the great Spanish humanist, Vives. She learned to speak excellent

Among the scholars whose works Mary studied were William Lily (above left) author of the first standard Latin grammar, and the Spanish philosopher and humanist, Vives (above).

19

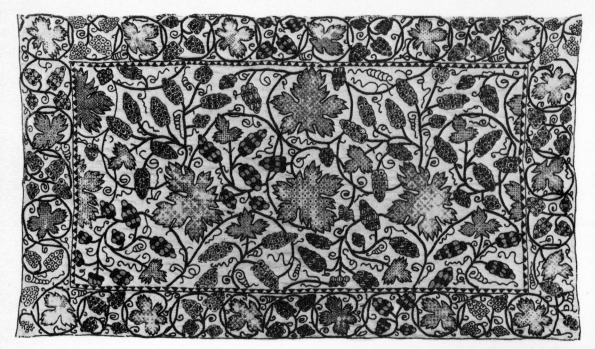

As well as enjoying an intellectual education far above that of most girls, Mary was proficient in the more usual feminine accomplishments – playing the spinet and embroidering.

TOP A sixteenth-century linen pillow cover embroidered in black silk.
ABOVE An Italian spinet of 1537.

French, Spanish and Latin, and to understand and read Italian, though in later life she did not usually venture to speak Italian, but replied in Latin when people spoke Italian to her. She was also taught the skills which every lady should know, such as riding side-saddle, sewing and embroidery; and she was taught to play the spinet, and encouraged to acquire her father's love of music. Many of her tutors have described how intelligent she was as a child. These panegyrics on Mary's intelligence, like those which were afterwards written about her brother Edward VI and her sister Elizabeth I, are not entirely reliable, because the writers may have been exaggerating in order to please the King; but there is every reason to believe that Mary, Edward and Elizabeth were all very intelligent children.

Henry VIII was very fond of Mary when she was a child, as he was of all his children, and very proud of her intellectual achievements and precocity. He often took the opportunity of introducing her to the foreign statesmen and papal legates who visited his Court. In February 1518, when Mary was just two years old, the Venetian Ambassador, Giustiniani, went to see Henry, accompanied by the famous musician Friar Dionisio Memo, the organist of St Mark's in Venice, whom Henry had invited to England. Mary was brought in, and Wolsey and Giustiniani kissed her hand, because, as Giustiniani reported to the Doge, 'the greatest marks of honour are paid to her universally, more than to the Queen herself'. Mary was just learning to talk. When she saw Memo in his friar's garb, she pointed at him, and said in English: 'Priest! Priest!' In later centuries, Protestant writers were to consider it significant that already at the age of two, Bloody Mary was under the nefarious influence of priests.

Although the daughters of kings were not considered to be suitable as sovereigns, they had an important role to play in state affairs by marrying foreign rulers with whom their fathers or brothers wished to make an alliance. These marriages, in which the personal inclination of the princes and princesses played very little part, were often arranged when the bride and bridegroom were still children. Henry VIII and Wolsey were already negotiating about Mary's marriage when she was a baby. The best match would have been for her to marry the Emperor Charles V. Charles was Mary's cousin, being the son

of Catherine of Aragon's sister; he was sixteen years older than
Mary. As Holy Roman Emperor, Charles was the overlord of
the independent sovereign princes and free cities of Germany,
and of many independent dukedoms of northern Italy; and as
well as being Holy Roman Emperor he was also King of Spain
and Naples, Archduke of Austria and Duke of Burgundy. The
duchy of Burgundy included the Netherlands – that is to say,
most of modern Belgium and Holland – and parts of eastern and
northern France.

England had for over a century been the ally of Burgundy,
both because of the thriving trade between England and the
Netherlands, which was the chief market for English wool, and
also because they were natural military allies against France.
Henry VIII and Wolsey continued this alliance with Charles V,
though from time to time they flirted with the King of France,
and lined up with France against the Emperor. In 1517, when
Anglo-French relations were very bad, Wolsey suddenly threw
out a hint to the French Ambassador that when the young King
of France, Francis I, had a son, it might be possible to arrange
a marriage between Francis's son and Mary. Relations between
Henry and Francis became more friendly next year, and they
negotiated a treaty under which they settled their disputes
about various international problems, and made a defensive
military alliance; and as Francis's Queen had just given birth
to a Dauphin, it was agreed that Mary should marry the
Dauphin when he was fourteen.

In September 1518 Francis I sent envoys to England to sign
the treaty and celebrate the betrothal of Francis the Dauphin
and Mary. The envoys were the Bishop of Paris and the young
Admiral of France, Bonnivet, who was a close friend of
Francis I's and had a great reputation for his gallantry and love
affairs. The Bishop of Paris and Bonnivet attended Mass with
Henry in St Paul's, and reported that the splendour of the
ceremony 'was too magnificent to describe'. It was followed by
a supper at Wolsey's house, 'the like of which, I fancy', wrote
the Venetian Ambassador, 'was never given either by Cleopatra
or Caligula'. Next day the French envoys went to Greenwich,
and there, on 5 October, in the Queen's great chamber, the
ceremony of betrothal took place.

Francis I had appointed Bonnivet to represent the Dauphin

22

A miniature of Francis I King of France, from a sixteenth-century manuscript. Negotiations between Francis and Wolsey led to Mary's betrothal to the infant Dauphin.

as his proxy at the ceremony; but Mary, though she was only two years and seven months old, took part in person. She was brought into the hall, which was lavishly decorated in the most expensive manner, and stood in front of her mother, who was standing at Henry's side before the throne. She was dressed in cloth-of-gold, and wore a black velvet cap which was adorned with many jewels. Bonnivet held her by the hand while Henry and Catherine gave their consent to the engagement. Wolsey had provided the engagement ring at his own expense as a gift to

24

the Princess; it was a small ring, specially made to fit her little hand, but contained a very large diamond. Wolsey put the ring on the fourth finger of Mary's right hand, pushing it on as far as the second joint in the finger; and then Bonnivet slipped it over the second joint to the base of the finger. Mary was then blessed by Wolsey and by the Papal Nuncio, and, after Wolsey had made a speech, the adults went off to another enormous banquet.

But Henry and Wolsey, despite their show of friendship with France, were always conscious that England's real interests lay in an alliance with the Netherlands and the Emperor. In the summer of 1520 Henry went to his town of Calais, which the English had held for nearly two hundred years, to meet Francis I at the lavish reception near Ardres, on the boundary of the French and English territories, which became known as the Field of Cloth-of-Gold. But on his way to France he had met Charles V at Canterbury; and as soon as his meeting with Francis was over, he met Charles again, at Gravelines, in the Emperor's territories. At these meetings, Henry and Charles made a secret treaty, under which Henry promised that he would not marry Mary to the Dauphin, and Charles promised not to marry Francis I's daughter; and they also agreed to explore the possibilities of negotiating a marriage between Charles and Mary. As Charles and Mary were cousins, their marriage was banned under the Canon Law; but there would be no difficulty about obtaining a papal dispensation for the marriage, because Pope Leo X was eager to do anything which would further the anti-French alliance of Charles and Henry.

In June 1522 Charles again visited England, and met Mary at Windsor. He was twenty-two, and she was six. In later years they were close allies, and all her life Mary looked to Charles for protection and advice; but this was the only time that they met. Before leaving England, Charles signed the marriage contract, under which it was agreed that he should marry Mary in six years' time, when Mary was twelve. Next year, Henry repudiated Mary's engagement to the Dauphin, and declared war on France in alliance with the Emperor.

Although the match between Charles and Mary was so eminently suitable, both Charles and Henry knew that many things might happen in six years to prevent the marriage from taking place. Charles knew that Henry and Wolsey were always capable of changing their foreign policy and making an alliance with Francis I against him, and he wanted to be sure that they would not repudiate the betrothal between him and Mary. He therefore suggested that Mary should be sent to his Court at once, so that she could be brought up in the countries whose Empress she was to be. Henry knew that if Mary was living in Charles's territories, his bargaining position would be weakened, and he refused to let her go to Charles's Court until after the marriage had taken place. Charles began to consider other suitable brides. He was tempted to repudiate his engagement to Mary in order to marry Princess Isabella of Portugal; he was

A sixteenth-century banquet from a woodcut in the *Treatise of Christoforo di Messisburgo*. Banquets were frequently the seal of goodwill at the end of diplomatic negotiations.

short of money at the moment, and the King of Portugal, with the wealth of the East Indies at his disposal, was offering a much larger dowry than Henry VIII. Meanwhile the Scottish government suggested that King James V of Scotland, who was a child only four years older than Mary, would be a suitable husband for her. Wolsey encouraged the Scots to think that Mary might marry James V, though really he had no intention of accepting James as Mary's husband, because the Emperor seemed to him to be the best match for Mary. At Wolsey's suggestion, Mary sent Charles a ring in the summer of 1525, when she was nine. The ring contained an emerald stone, which was the emblem of constancy.

In 1525, relations between Henry and Charles became strained, and Charles decided to break off the engagement with Mary and marry Princess Isabella of Portugal. Henry and Wolsey were disappointed, but they did not wish to quarrel too seriously with Charles, and they agreed to release him from the contract.

Henry VIII was now seriously worried about the succession to the crown. Catherine of Aragon was forty, and it was becoming increasingly clear that she would not produce another child. But Henry Fitzroy, his son by Elizabeth Blount, was growing up to be a healthy boy; and Henry began to wonder whether it would be possible to legitimise him, either by papal dispensation or by Act of Parliament, so that he could become King when Henry died. In 1525, when the boy was six, Henry created him Duke of Richmond, which was a high mark of honour, because the Richmond title had been borne by Henry VII before he became King. The boy was given a princely household, and the King issued an order laying down that the Duke of Richmond was to have precedence, after Henry himself, over everyone else in the realm, including Mary. Catherine of Aragon resented this very much. She was indignant that Elizabeth Blount's bastard should be given precedence over her own daughter, and she rightly feared that this might be a prelude to giving the Duke of Richmond the title of Prince of Wales, and making him heir to the throne instead of Mary.

But very soon afterwards Henry took a step in the opposite direction. He sent Mary to Ludlow Castle, and set her up there with an imposing establishment of her own. Ludlow, on the

27

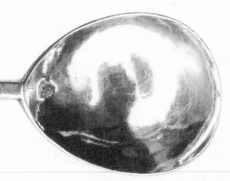

Three examples of Tudor
craftsmanship.
LEFT A silver chalice made
for the Peacock family in
the 1550s. OPPOSITE An
early sixteenth-century
bowl of serpentine marble
in silver gilt and a silver
apostle spoon.

borders of Wales, was traditionally one of the residences of the Prince of Wales, from where the Prince, with his Council, could govern the Welsh Marches. Mary, who was only nine years old, was too young to govern Wales, and was not given either the title of Princess of Wales or any share in the government of the principality; but sending her to Ludlow was interpreted as the first step to prepare the people for her future role as heir to the throne and ultimately as Queen of England.

Meanwhile negotiations were continuing about Mary's marriage, which again was to be used as an instrument of Wolsey's foreign policy. In 1525 Charles v defeated Francis I at the battle of Pavia, where he took Francis prisoner, and

Cardinal Wolsey and his suite in progress. The great cardinal was the most powerful man in the kingdom after Henry but was to fall from favour when he failed to win Henry a speedy divorce from Catherine.

became, for the moment, unchallenged master of Europe; but Wolsey, in order to restore the international balance of power, made an alliance with France. Francis I's wife had died some years before, and while he was Charles's prisoner he signed a treaty with Charles under which he agreed to marry Charles's sister Eleanor, and to marry the Dauphin to Eleanor's daughter by her first marriage with the King of Portugal. But as soon as Francis was released from captivity, and back in Paris, Wolsey suggested that he should break off his engagement to Eleanor and marry Mary. So Mary, who eight years before had been solemnly betrothed to Francis's son, the Dauphin, was now to marry Francis himself, though he was twenty-two years older then she, and only three years younger than her father. Francis hesitated to agree, fearing that the Emperor would renew the war if Francis broke off his engagement to his sister; and as this might also apply if the Dauphin broke off his betrothal and married Mary, Francis suggested that Mary should be engaged to his second son, Henry, Duke of Orleans, who was three years younger than Mary, and afterwards became King Henry II of France. Wolsey would have preferred to force a rupture between France and the Emperor by marrying Mary to Francis himself; but he agreed to make a treaty with Francis by which she was to marry either Francis, or, if this proved impossible, the Duke of Orleans.

In April 1527 Mary was summoned to come to Court from Ludlow to meet the French envoys whom Francis had sent to sign the treaty. She was eleven years old, and was able to play a more active part in the festivities than she had done during her first two betrothal ceremonies. The head of the French delegation, the Viscount of Turenne, was charmed with her. She spoke to him in French, Latin and Italian, she danced with him, and played for him on the spinet. He reported that she would grow up to be a beautiful woman and that she was very intelligent. The proceedings culminated in a great banquet and party at Greenwich. It cost £8,000, which is the equivalent of about £800,000 in terms of prices today.

But by this time, Henry VIII had fallen passionately in love with Anne Boleyn.

2 The Bastard

Daughter 1527-36

ANNE BOLEYN, LIKE HER SISTER MARY, had come to Court. Although she had some deformity in one hand – her enemies said that she had six fingers – she was very attractive to men, and by 1527 the King was more deeply in love with her than he had ever been with her elder sister; but Anne, either from virtue, coquetry or ambition, refused to become his mistress, and made it clear that she would only comply if Henry made her his wife and Queen of England. The prospect of marrying Anne, and of her giving him a legitimate son, finally convinced Henry that his conscientious scruples about the validity of his marriage to Catherine were justified; and by 1527 he had firmly persuaded himself that Catherine had never been his lawful wife, and that Mary was illegitimate.

He set about trying to persuade the Pope to declare that the papal dispensation of 1503, which had permitted him to marry his brother's widow, was void. In ordinary circumstances the Pope might have been persuaded to do this in order to oblige the powerful King of England; but Charles V, who was angry with Henry because Henry had made an alliance with France and had declared war on him, used all his influence to prevent the Pope from granting the divorce. Pope Clement VII was a weak man who always tried to postpone an embarrassing decision for as long as possible. He would have preferred not to offend Henry, but under no circumstances could he afford to offend Charles. So he found one pretext after another to adjourn the proceedings in the divorce case, and continued to do this for seven years.

From the beginning, Mary was on her mother's side in the dispute. She was aged eleven when the divorce negotiations began. As a young Princess, she naturally saw more of her mother than of her father, and was very fond of her. She lived in the daily company of Catherine and of Catherine's Spanish ladies-in-waiting, who championed the Queen's cause. She had also her own motives for opposing the divorce, which would have the effect of making her a bastard. As the divorce proceedings dragged on, Henry became more and more irritated at Catherine's refusal to retire peacefully into a convent, which seemed to him to be disloyal and unpatriotic on her part; and in his resentment he began to treat her very badly, slighting her in public and eventually ordering her to hand over her

PREVIOUS PAGES An early sixteenth-century carving of the royal arms of England as borne by Henry VIII.

34

Anne Boleyn, who so
bewitched King Henry
that he was prepared to
break with Rome in order
to divorce Catherine
and marry her.

jewellery to Anne Boleyn. But Catherine was still in love with
Henry. She declared that she was willing to obey him in all
things, but remained patiently obstinate about the divorce. All
this made Mary more devoted than ever to her mother, and
more opposed to her father's attitude.

One aspect of the divorce proceedings was very unpleasant
for Catherine and Mary. Henry's lawyers tried to find all kinds
of legal technicalities which would invalidate the papal
dispensation of 1503. One possible way of doing this was to
argue that Pope Julius II had only granted the dispensation

because he believed that the marriage between Prince Arthur and Catherine had not been consummated – though this was very debatable, in view of the wording of the dispensation – but that, in fact, the marriage had been consummated, and the dispensation had therefore been obtained by false pretences, and was void. A public trial was held at Blackfriars monastery in London in 1529, when Mary was thirteen, at which many elderly courtiers gave evidence to show that the marriage had been consummated twenty-eight years before, though Catherine stoutly denied it, and stated that Henry, at least, knew that she had come to him as a virgin. Some of the evidence given was very sordid, and this may have been one of the reasons why Mary grew up with a strong aversion to sex.

The divorce proceedings aroused a great deal of feeling in England. Most of the common people, particularly the women, supported Catherine. They were not interested in the niceties of the legal and canonical questions, but felt that this was a case where the King wished to get rid of a loyal wife to whom he had been married for twenty years in order to marry a young adventuress. When Catherine went out, she was cheered by the women in the street. Mary, too, was very popular with the people. In 1528 it was reported that the citizens of London were saying that they would not accept anyone as their King after Henry's death except the husband of the Lady Mary.

This was probably one of the reasons why Henry, in October 1528, thought of a new solution to the problem of the succession. This was for the Pope to give a dispensation for Mary to marry her bastard half-brother, the Duke of Richmond, and to legitimise Richmond, so that Richmond could succeed to the throne as King, with Mary as his Queen. When Henry suggested this to the Pope, Clement hoped that this might be a way out of his difficulties about Catherine's divorce. He offered to grant the dispensation for Richmond to marry Mary if Henry gave up his attempt to divorce Catherine. Henry was too infatuated with Anne Boleyn to agree to this bargain.

Anne herself had another plan for Mary. She suggested to Henry that he should marry Mary to the Duke of Norfolk's son, Henry Howard, Earl of Surrey, who was then aged ten, two years younger than Mary, and later grew up to be a well-known gallant and a charming poet. Surrey was the last of many political prisoners to suffer death at Henry's orders; he was beheaded in 1547, eight days before Henry died. Anne Boleyn had her own reasons for proposing this match. Norfolk was her uncle, and though he afterwards presided at her trial and sentenced her to death, at this time he was, as usual, ingratiating himself with the influential party at Court, and was supporting Anne. Anne thought that if Norfolk's son married Mary, it

Pope Clement VII, whose fear of offending either Henry or Charles V allowed the divorce proceedings to drag on for seven years.

37

would be an advancement for a family connexion, and that if Mary married a subject who was her inferior in rank, it was much less likely that Henry would allow her to succeed to the throne. Mary's marriage to Surrey would therefore help to clear the way for the children whom Anne hoped to bear to Henry after she had married him. But Henry would not agree that Mary should marry Surrey.

Although Catherine of Aragon and Mary were so popular with the majority of the people of England, there was one group of Henry's subjects who supported him in the divorce proceedings. These were the religious reformers who were then usually called Lutherans, but who, before Mary died, had become known as Protestants. The doctrines of the Protestants had originated in England about a hundred and fifty years before, when Wycliffe expounded them at the end of the fourteenth century. His followers, the Lollards, had been effectively suppressed by persecution in the reign of Henry IV, but had never been completely eradicated, and the movement revived after Martin Luther, in Germany, denounced the abuses of the Church in 1517.

In 1530 there were not many Protestants in England. They were strongest among the intellectuals, which, in the sixteenth century, meant chiefly theologians in holy orders. They also had some support among educated laymen, such as barristers and merchants. Apart from these, there were a number of extreme Protestants among the more unusual, or unstable, individuals of the artisan and labouring classes. These individuals sometimes erected stools in the street, or in their gardens, and preached their own individual religion to the passers-by, although it was illegal for anyone to preach without a licence from the bishop of the diocese. Other extremists committed acts which outraged the majority of the people, such as mutilating images in churches, or desecrating the Host, for which they were severely punished if they were caught. Nearly all the Protestants were in south-eastern England; they were almost unknown in the north and west.

The Church condemned the Protestant doctrine as heresy. Ever since the thirteenth century it had been accepted that the punishment for heresy was burning alive, and in England an Act of Parliament of 1401 enacted that if anyone was

OPPOSITE The remains of statues of St Michael and the Virgin Mary in the church of St Michael, Coslany, Norwich which were mutilated by extreme Protestants in Henry's reign.

condemned as a heretic by the Church courts, the King could sign an order to have him burned without further process, though if the heretic recanted, he was nearly always pardoned after performing some minor penance. Burning was also the punishment for a few other offenders, such as witches, wives who murdered their husbands, and women guilty of high treason. Men who committed high treason were hanged, drawn and quartered; but the King could commute the sentence on both men and women traitors to beheading, and always did so if they were of noble birth.

Henry VIII, like all other Christian kings, burned heretics who had been condemned by the Church and who refused to recant; but when the Protestants heard that Henry was eager to annul his marriage to Catherine, and was trying to invalidate the papal dispensation which had permitted him to marry her, they came to his assistance. They argued that the Pope had no power to grant any dispensation if it conflicted with the law of God, by which they meant anything laid down in the Bible; and, basing themselves on a biblical text, they pronounced that the Pope had no power to permit a man to marry his brother's widow. This drew Henry a little closer to the Protestants. He continued to burn Protestants, but at the same time he took a few of the more moderate and discreet Protestants into his service and used them for his own purposes. It was widely rumoured that Anne Boleyn and her father were Lutherans, though the extent of their Protestantism was probably exaggerated by their enemies.

Mary, like all other princes and princesses in Europe, had been brought up as a Catholic, and taught to believe that Lutherans were heretics who should be burned if they persisted in their error. She was also influenced by the fact that her mother, and her mother's Spanish ladies-in-waiting, were particularly devout Catholics. The Protestant support for the King's divorce, and the alleged Lutheranism of the Boleyns, were additional reasons for Mary to be strongly Catholic and anti-Protestant.

Although the Protestants had very little support among the people of England in 1530, there was one point on which their thinking was in line with public opinion. There was a good deal of resentment against the papal authority over the Church of

England, not on doctrinal grounds, but because the people objected to the amount of money that had to be paid to officials in Rome, and to the delays involved in obtaining the necessary legal authority from Rome in ecclesiastical matters, and because of the increasing nationalist feeling in England. The English hated foreigners, and anything which savoured of foreign domination over England.

In the last years of Henry VIII's reign, and under Edward VI, there was a powerful body of opinion in the Church, at Court and in the country, which was Catholic but anti-Papist. The most prominent leader of this party was Stephen Gardiner, Bishop of Winchester, who afterwards, in Mary's reign, became her Lord Chancellor, but in 1530 was energetically working for Henry's divorce. But Gardiner's Cambridge colleague, Thomas Cranmer, who had been enrolled in the King's service by Gardiner because of his support for the divorce, was a moderate Protestant, who had secretly married a Lutheran wife in Germany. The marriage of priests was forbidden by the Catholic Church, and severely punished, but it was permitted by Protestant doctrines.

For four years, Henry continued to live with Catherine while he tried to persuade the Pope to annul the marriage. Mary lived with them at Court, being constantly together with her mother. But Henry thought that Catherine was a bad influence on Mary, and was enlisting her support in the divorce case. He therefore decided to separate them. He set up a separate establishment for Mary at Newhall, near Chelmsford in Essex; but though Mary lived there sometimes, she spent as much time as possible with her mother at Court. Then suddenly in July 1531, when the Court was at Windsor, Henry told Catherine that his conscience would no longer permit him to live with his deceased brother's wife, and, without saying goodbye, he moved to Woodstock. He never saw Catherine again. Mary was ordered to go and live at Richmond. Some months later, when Henry returned to Windsor, he ordered Catherine to leave before he arrived, and go to the palace of the Moor in Hertfordshire, while Mary lived mostly at Newhall. Mary was very unhappy at being separated from her mother, though she and Catherine found some consolation in writing very often to each other.

Richmond Palace, drawn
by Wyngaerde, where
Mary was sent in 1531 to be
separated from her mother.

By this time Anne Boleyn, whom Henry had created Lady Marquis of Pembroke in her own right, had at last agreed to become Henry's mistress, and was openly cohabiting with him. In December 1532 she became pregnant. This might be the son and heir for which Henry had waited for so long; but if he was to be legitimate, they must be married at once. In January 1533 Henry was secretly married to Anne. He then appointed Cranmer Archbishop of Canterbury, and ordered him to sit as a judge and try his divorce case in the priory at Dunstable. Catherine refused to recognise Cranmer's court or to appear before it; but Cranmer gave judgment that her marriage to Henry had always been unlawful, and that Mary was illegitimate. He made no attempt to act impartially, and was writing to Henry, before and during the trial, promising that he would give judgment for Henry in time for Anne Boleyn to be crowned Queen on Whit Sunday. On 7 September Anne gave birth to her child. To the intense disappointment of Henry and Anne, and to the joy of Catherine's supporters, it was a girl. The child became the future Queen Elizabeth I.

In March 1534, nearly a year after Cranmer's judgment at Dunstable, the papal court in Rome gave final judgment for Catherine in the divorce case. The judgment was not recognised in England. It was a great consolation to Catherine and Mary, but otherwise had no effect whatever.

As a result of Cranmer's judgment, Catherine was no longer entitled to call herself Queen. Anne Boleyn was the Queen, and Catherine was to be known as the Princess Dowager, being the widow of Prince Arthur, her only lawful husband. Catherine and Mary bitterly resented this title, and refused to use it or to respond to it. But Henry was determined to compel all his subjects to recognise his marriage to Anne Boleyn, and to overthrow the spiritual supremacy of the Pope. Parliament passed an Act which declared that the Pope had no authority in England, and was in future not to be called Pope, but the Bishop of Rome; and another Act declared that anyone who was asked to do so must swear an oath that he believed that Anne Boleyn's children were legitimate and the heirs to the crown, and that Henry was 'Supreme Head, next under Christ, of this Church of England'. These two oaths were known as the Oath of the Succession and the Oath of Supremacy. A refusal to swear the Oath of the Succession was punishable by imprisonment for life; a refusal to swear the Oath of Supremacy was high treason, and punishable by death.

Henry ordered that everyone in the country who held any kind of official position was to be required to swear the oaths. Only a handful refused to swear. These included John Fisher, Bishop of Rochester; Sir Thomas More, a former Lord Chancellor and an old personal friend of Henry's; and five Carthusian priors and monks. They were executed in the summer of 1535. The King allowed Fisher and More to be beheaded; the monks, after being treated with great cruelty in prison, were hanged, drawn and quartered.

The situation had become very difficult and dangerous for Catherine and Mary. As they were both Henry's subjects, they, too, could be required at any time to swear the Oath of the Succession and the Oath of Supremacy. They were always expecting to be asked to swear, and had decided to refuse, and suffer the consequences. But Henry hesitated to enforce the law against Catherine and Mary, because he was afraid of angering the Emperor Charles V, whose ambassador, Eustace Chapuys, was using all his influence on their behalf. Chapuys was a very skilful diplomat, and Catherine and Mary were in close touch with him, though this had to be kept secret for fear of angering Henry. They followed Chapuys's advice in all matters. This was another factor which influenced Mary's attitude for the rest of her life. She came to think of the Emperor as her protector and her only powerful friend.

Henry tried to break the resistance of Catherine and Mary by acts of petty persecution. In April 1533, a month before Cranmer gave judgment in the divorce case, Henry sent a message to Mary to inform her abruptly that he had married Anne Boleyn. Mary was taken aback, but quickly recovered herself. According to Chapuys, 'like a wise woman as she is, she dissembled the matter, showing herself glad'. But worse was to come. Later the same day she received another message from Henry, telling her that she must not write to her mother in future. This was a heavy blow to Mary. She asked permission to be allowed to write one last letter to Catherine, which Henry's officials could read and then deliver; but this request was refused.

In September, after the birth of Elizabeth, Henry sent Lord

PIO AC CATHOLICO LECTORI · S·

Hussey to tell Mary that she must hand over her jewels to Anne Boleyn's baby, and must not call herself Princess, or use the style of a Princess. Her servants were to remove the gold from their uniforms, and dress in humbler attire. Mary handed over the jewels, but refused to renounce her title of Princess or remove her servants' insignia of rank. She told Hussey that she was sure that her father would not expect her to comply with such an order unless he had personally communicated it to her. When Henry heard what had happened, he sent the Dean of the Chapel Royal, Sampson, to tell Mary that the King was surprised 'that she, forgetting her filial duty and allegiance', had attempted, in spite of the command conveyed to her by Lord Hussey, 'arrogantly to usurp the title of Princess, pretending to be heir apparent', and that 'she has worthily deserved the King's high displeasure and punishment by law'.

On 14 December Henry sent the Duke of Norfolk to tell Mary that she was to move to Hatfield and join the Princess Elizabeth's household. A few days later, she was taken there with only two of her own attendants to accompany her. When she arrived at Hatfield, Norfolk asked her whether she would go and pay her respects to the Princess. 'She replied', wrote Chapuys, 'that she knew no other Princess in England except herself, and that the daughter of Lady Pembroke had no such title', but that 'since the King her father acknowledged her to be his, she might call her sister, as she called the Duke of Richmond brother'.

Mary's attitude angered Henry. He insisted that Mary, as his illegitimate daughter, would have to give precedence to the Princess, and accept a position of inferiority to the child whom she regarded as Anne Boleyn's bastard. In the sixteenth century, when everyone attached so much importance to precedence and rank, this was a profound humiliation to Mary. Elizabeth's household was in the charge of Lady Shelton, who was Anne Boleyn's aunt, and Mary was placed under her authority. The King told Lady Shelton that if Mary was troublesome, Lady Shelton was to give her a good beating. But though Mary was often troublesome, from Henry's point of view, Lady Shelton never beat her, and on one occasion was reprimanded by the Duke of Norfolk for treating Mary too leniently.

Elizabeth's household, like the King's Court, moved from

place to place quite frequently, residing in turn at a number of houses in the neighbourhood of London. The move from one house to the next was a formal and stately 'progress' at the rate of ten or fifteen miles a day. In the sixteenth century, the English roads were in a worse state than they had been for many centuries; it was only in the seventeenth century that the first improvements in road surfaces were made. Apart from king's messengers travelling 'in post' with relays of horses, travellers rarely went more than thirty miles a day, and persons of higher rank thought it necessary for their dignity to travel more slowly, and only cover about half this distance. Because of this, the Tudor kings could never go very far from London. Henry VIII visited the northern part of his kingdom on only one occasion, and Mary, like Elizabeth I, stayed all her life in the south of England. Mary never went further west than Ludlow or further north than Norwich.

As a member of Elizabeth's household, Mary was expected to accompany the baby Princess on her progress, which meant that Mary would have to ride behind her, in an inferior position in the procession, and be publicly seen by the onlookers all along the road to be occupying this position of inferiority. This made Mary very angry. When she was told that she must ride behind the litter in which Elizabeth and her nurse would be travelling, she refused to go. Lady Shelton told her that in this case she would be put in another litter, if necessary by force, and made to follow Elizabeth's litter. Mary still refused, whereupon Lady Shelton ordered some gentlemen to seize her and carry her by force to the litter and hold her there during the journey. Mary knew that this problem would arise again whenever Elizabeth moved to another house, and she asked Chapuys what to do, because, somehow or other – by what means we do not know – she managed to keep secretly in touch with him. The Ambassador, as always, gave her good advice. He told her that the next time she was ordered to ride behind Elizabeth's litter on a progress, she should protest against the order, 'boldly', but 'with her accustomed modesty', but should not go to the length of allowing herself to be put into a litter by physical force.

Mary followed Chapuys's advice, and on one occasion actually managed to turn the circumstances to her own advantage. Elizabeth was moving to the south of the river, which involved

Sixteenth-century ornaments such as Mary
was forced to hand over to Elizabeth:
ABOVE Pendants and crosses possibly of
Spanish origin.
OPPOSITE A hairpin made of carved bone.

The Succession of
Henry VIII, painted in
Elizabeth's reign, shows
Mary and Philip followed
by Mars, the god of war,
and Elizabeth followed by
Flora and the fruits of
prosperity. Edward VI
kneels beside his father.

Septentrio

crossing the Thames in a barge. When they started out, Mary rode behind Elizabeth's litter as she was supposed to do; but a little while before they came to the river, she suddenly spurred her horse forward, before anyone could stop her, and rode past Elizabeth's litter, galloping ahead and reaching the barge before any of the Princess's cortège arrived. She thereupon got into the barge, and occupied the place of honour in it. When the others arrived, they found Mary in possession, and apparently left her in the seat of honour, perhaps because they did not wish to use physical force to remove her in full view of the public who had gathered to see the royal party.

Mary also tried to use the occasion of these humiliating progresses to get a glimpse of Chapuys, even though she would not have the opportunity of speaking to him. On one occasion she secretly asked Chapuys to station himself somewhere along the route by which Elizabeth's progress was to travel, so that she could see him for a moment. Chapuys discovered that she would be travelling up the river by barge, and took up his position near a house in the fields between Greenwich and

London. As the barge passed, Mary came up on deck and
looked at Chapuys. She made no sign of recognition, but stood
there with her eyes fixed on him until he was out of sight. It
was the first time for many months that this girl of eighteen,
who was held as a virtual prisoner in her enemy's house, had
been able to look at a friend.

Once, when Mary was in Elizabeth's household at Eltham,
the Queen, Anne Boleyn, was there too. Anne made no attempt
to speak to Mary, but they both attended Mass with all the
household in the chapel in the palace. Mary had no objection to
this, because although Henry had repudiated the papal authority,
he had made no change at all in the doctrine of the Eucharist,
and the service of the Mass was the same as it was everywhere in
Catholic Europe. At the end of the service, Mary curtsied to the
altar as she left the chapel. Anne did not notice it, but one of her
ladies did, and told Anne that Mary, as she left the chapel, had
curtsied to Anne. Anne decided to make a gesture of reconciliation, and sent the lady-in-waiting to Mary. The lady said to
Mary: 'The Queen salutes your Grace with much affection and

craves pardon, understanding that at your parting from the oratory you made a curtsey to her, which, if she had seen, she would have answered you with the like; and she desires that this may be an entrance of friendly correspondence which your Grace shall find completely to be embraced on her part.' But Mary was in no mood to make any kind of reconciliation with Anne; and she replied to the lady-in-waiting:

> It is not possible that the Queen can send me such a message; nor is it fit she should, nor can it be so sudden, Her Majesty being so far from this place. You would have said, the Lady Anne Boleyn, for I can acknowledge no other Queen but my mother, nor esteem them my friends who are not hers. And for the reverence that I made, it was to the altar, to her Maker and mine; and so they are deceived, and deceive her who tell her otherwise.

When Anne heard what Mary had said, she became very angry, and said 'that one day she would pull down this high spirit'.

Henry himself sometimes visited his daughter Elizabeth. On these occasions, he refused to see Mary, although he had been so fond of her when she was a child, and gave orders that she was to be confined to her room during his visit. Once, when Henry was visiting Elizabeth at Hatfield, Mary, who as usual had been ordered to stay in her room while he was in the house, asked permission to see him; but he refused. Next morning, hearing that Henry was about to depart, Mary walked out on to the battlements of the tower to look at him. After he had mounted his horse, and was on the point of leaving, he looked up and saw Mary on the tower. He saluted her, and rode away.

In September 1534 Mary fell seriously ill. To everyone's surprise, Henry showed great concern, and not only sent his own physician to attend to her, but allowed Catherine of Aragon to visit her. Catherine and Mary had not met for more than two years, and had not been allowed to write to each other for nearly eighteen months; but now they had a brief and happy reunion, not knowing that they would never meet again. (Nearly all the biographies of Catherine and Mary have stated that mother and daughter never met again after their separation in 1532; but Chapuys wrote that they were allowed to meet on this occasion in September 1534.) Mary recovered slowly, but in February had a set-back. Catherine wrote to Henry and asked him to send Mary to her, so that she could nurse her 'with my own hands'. Henry's kindness in allowing them to meet in September had encouraged false hopes; but her request was refused.

Mary recovered her health, but her anxieties increased. Her greatest fear was that Henry might at any time require her to swear the Oath of the Succession and the Oath of Supremacy, with the terrible consequences if she refused to do so. Catherine of Aragon believed that she and Mary would soon be executed. One day, Mary overheard some of Lady Shelton's ladies talking among themselves. The ladies said that they had heard that the King had decided to cut off Mary's head if she refused to take the oaths. Mary was seriously alarmed, and she felt that her only hope was to let Chapuys know at once, so that he and the Emperor could use their influence to save her. But at the moment she could not think of a way of getting into touch with Chapuys immediately.

It so happened that Mary's old tutor, who had taught her Latin when she was a child, came to see her. As always when Mary received visitors, the ladies of Elizabeth's household were present; but Mary knew that the ladies did not speak Latin. In the course of the conversation, she told the tutor that she had completely forgotten all the Latin that he had taught her, and that if she were to say something to him in Latin now, it would be such bad Latin that he would not understand it. The tutor said that he could not believe this, and asked her to say something in Latin so that he could judge for himself. Mary then said, in Latin: 'The King is thinking of cutting off my head. Tell the Emperor's Ambassador.' The tutor was so surprised and shocked that for a moment he was at a loss what to say; but he recovered himself, and coolly said that this was indeed not good Latin. As soon as he left Mary, he went to Chapuys's house, and told Chapuys what Mary had said. Chapuys decided to let Henry know that he had heard a rumour that Mary was to be put to death, while not saying anything to let Henry think that he had been in touch with Mary herself. He said that he had heard a rumour in London that Mary was to be executed, and was sure that Henry would wish to deny the truth of this rumour. Chapuys afterwards believed that Henry had been deterred from proceeding against Mary because he knew that the Emperor had been warned of his plan.

Chapuys was so worried about the danger to Catherine and Mary that he wished to arrange for them to escape abroad to the Emperor's territories. He managed to communicate with them about this in the greatest secrecy. He had to be very careful, because he knew that Henry would be determined to prevent either Catherine or Mary escaping abroad, and becoming, perhaps, a centre of plotting and opposition to him at the Emperor's Court; and Chapuys was sure that if Henry found out that he was planning their escape, it would not only cause a serious diplomatic incident, but would greatly increase the danger to the lives of Catherine and Mary. Catherine refused to try to escape. She had always adopted an attitude of Griselda-like patience and wifely submission in the face of the ill-treatment to which Henry subjected her – an attitude which only exasperated Henry still more – and she felt that she must prove that she was Henry's obedient wife and subject by remaining in his kingdom. But she agreed that Mary should try to escape.

Mary was eager to make the attempt. Chapuys wrote to the Emperor that Mary was so keen to escape that she would be prepared to cross the Channel in a sieve if he advised her to do it. But Mary realised the difficulties. She sent a secret message to Chapuys, telling him that it would be useless for her to try to escape at night, because she was always very carefully guarded at night in the houses where she stayed. It would be easier for her to escape when she went out walking during the day. At that time she was staying at Eltham, and she thought that if some horsemen came upon her there, when she was out walking, bringing a horse for her to ride, they could gallop to Gravesend and sail away to the Netherlands before the English authorities could stop them. She suggested that the horsemen should carry her off after she had made a show of resistance; this, she thought, would make things a little less dangerous for her if she were caught, and would be less offensive to her father's honour than if it were publicly known that his daughter had tried to escape from his realm.

A little while later, Mary suggested another plan to Chapuys. She now thought that she could, after all, escape from the house at night if he sent her something with which she could drug the women of the household who watched over her. If she drugged them, she would be able to walk out of the house into the

OPPOSITE Charles V at the battle of Mühlberg by Titian. The Emperor's sympathy for Mary prevented Henry VIII and later Edward VI from treating her as harshly as they wished.

57

garden. She would then have to take the risk of walking past Lady Shelton's window; but if she succeeded in doing this without being seen, she could easily open, or break down, the garden gate, and get out into the lane, where Chapuys's horsemen would be waiting for her.

At the same time as she pressed Chapuys to arrange for her escape, she made it plain that, in her opinion, this was only a second-best course; what she really wished was that the Emperor should invade England, and 'rescue innumerable souls from perdition'. In the summer of 1535, at the time of the executions of Fisher, More and the Carthusian monks, Mary wrote to Chapuys and begged him to urge the Emperor 'for the service of God, the peace of Christendom, the honour of my father, and compassion for poor afflicted souls', to 'take brief order and apply a remedy'. Charles at this time was campaigning against the Turks in North Africa; but Mary told Chapuys that if Charles set matters right in England, he would be performing 'a service most agreeable to Almighty God, nor will he acquire less fame and glory to himself than the conquest of Tunis or the whole of Africa'. If this letter had fallen into Henry's hands, he might well have had Mary executed for high treason.

Chapuys was anxious about the escape project. He was afraid of the consequences if the attempt were unsuccessful, and he thought that the very fact that, according to Mary, it would be so easy for her to escape from the house, and that she had been lodged in a place near the sea, might be because Henry was laying a trap for her in order to tempt her into making an unsuccessful attempt to escape. But he was almost persuaded to agree by Mary's enthusiasm for the plan, and wrote to Charles asking for instructions. Charles was very discouraging. He pointed out the grave risks involved, and said that even if the enterprise might be attempted one day, it should not be tried at the present time. Charles sincerely wished to do the best he could for Catherine and Mary, and was very concerned about the dangers which they would run if Mary tried to escape; but perhaps he was also influenced by the fact that, from his own point of view, it could have been very embarrassing diplomatically to have Mary residing in his territories, if ever his relations with England took a turn for the better.

At Christmas 1535 Catherine fell dangerously ill at her house at Kimbolton in Northamptonshire. Mary was not allowed to visit her or write to her, and Catherine was not allowed to write a last letter to Mary. Chapuys, who was allowed to visit her on her deathbed, suspected that Henry had poisoned her, but this is very unlikely. She died on 7 January.

There was no doubt that, politically, her death removed many difficulties for Henry, and also for Charles v. All papal supporters now admitted that Henry's marriage to Catherine had been dissolved by death in 1536 if not by divorce in 1533. In their eyes, Henry was now a widower, and though he was cohabiting in sin with his concubine Anne Boleyn, he was free to marry again. His chief minister, Thomas Cromwell, who had always been eager to re-establish friendly relations with the Emperor, had a talk with Chapuys three months after Catherine's death. He asked Chapuys whether, now that Catherine was dead, he thought that Catholic Europe would ever be prepared to recognise Anne Boleyn as Henry's lawful wife. Chapuys replied that he thought that they would never recognise Anne as Henry's wife, but might be persuaded to recognise someone else as his wife. He had chosen just the right moment to drop the hint, because he knew that Henry was tiring of Anne Boleyn, and had fallen in love with Jane Seymour, the daughter of a knight of Wiltshire.

Anne Boleyn had had the misfortune to be unable to give Henry a son. Their marital relations became very strained, with fatal results for Anne. In May 1536 she was suddenly arrested and charged with committing adultery with three men, one of whom was her own brother, and with plotting to murder Henry. She and her reputed lovers were all executed. On the day before Anne was beheaded, Cranmer annulled her marriage to Henry after a farcical trial. He did not give the reason for his decision, but it was probably that her marriage to Henry was void under Canon Law because Anne's sister had been Henry's mistress before he married Anne.

Mary and all her supporters were delighted at the fall and execution of Anne Boleyn, though Mary prayed for Anne's soul. They had always attributed their troubles, and the schism and heresy, to Anne's influence; and they believed all the accusations of adultery and incest against her, and regarded her conduct as an example of Protestant immorality. At first they hoped that Henry would sever all connexion with the Protestants; but they were disappointed. Cromwell, who was sympathetic to Protestant doctrines, became more powerful than ever after Anne Boleyn's death, and during 1536 and 1537 various Protestant innovations were introduced into the doctrine and practice of the Church of England. But the old Catholic Mass was retained without alteration.

Apart from anything else, Henry had found Protestantism profitable. In February 1536 he had suppressed most of the monasteries in England, and the remaining houses were suppressed three years later. The ostensible reason for suppressing them was the grossly immoral way in which the monks and nuns behaved in the houses, though these allegations of immorality were almost certainly exaggerated. Henry seized the property of the monasteries without compensation, gave part of it to special favourites and sold the rest at market value to country gentlemen in the neighbourhood, or to speculators who resold it at a profit to the gentlemen. Henry not only made a good profit out of the transaction, but also ensured that the gentlemen who had bought the property had a vested interest in supporting the dissolution of the monasteries. Mary, like other Catholic supporters, was distressed at the suppression of the religious houses; but it was the only one of Henry's Protestant measures that she was unable to reverse when she became Queen, because of the opposition of the gentlemen who had bought the property. The dissolution of the monasteries, unlike most of Henry's Protestant innovations, was accepted with real enthusiasm by the gentlemen and merchants in the House of Commons, and was popular with many of the English people, in the south if not in the north, because the monks had a reputation for being bad landlords. But within a few years, even ardent Protestants were admitting that however bad the monks had been, the new landlords who had bought the monastic property were even worse.

The death of Catherine of Aragon and the fall of Anne Boleyn opened up real prospects of an improvement in Mary's position. By annulling Henry's marriage to Anne, Cranmer had made Elizabeth as much a bastard as Mary; Henry's illegitimate son, the Duke of Richmond, died in 1536; and Henry now hoped for a legitimate heir from Jane Seymour,

A miniature of Catherine of Aragon attributed to L. von Horenboot.

whom he married eleven days after Anne was executed. Chapuys therefore suggested to Cromwell that Henry might agree to be reconciled to Mary and allow her to come to Court. Cromwell himself was in favour of the scheme; but he found it very difficult to persuade Henry to agree. Eventually Henry said that he would forgive Mary if she would sign articles repudiating the papal supremacy and admitting that her mother's marriage to him had been unlawful. He sent the Duke of Norfolk and other Privy Councillors to Mary, who was living at Hunsdon in Hertfordshire, to require her to sign the articles.

But Mary felt that to sign the articles would be a betrayal of her mother. The two of them had agreed that they would suffer death rather than swear the Oaths of the Succession and Supremacy, and Mary revolted at the idea of betraying their sacred resolve now that Catherine was dead. When Norfolk and the other Privy Councillors arrived at Hunsdon, she refused to sign the articles. The Privy Councillors did not know what to

OVERLEAF LEFT Princess Mary painted by an unknown artist in 1541.

OVERLEAF RIGHT A A portrait of Edward VI, attributed to Guillim Stretes.

ANNO DNI   1544

LADI MARI   DOVGHTER TO
THE MOST   VERTVOVS PRINCE
KING HENRI   THE EIGHT

THE AGE OF   XXVIII YERES

do, and were probably a little worried about the consequences to themselves if they failed to get Mary to submit. At first they tried to reason with her; but when they found that their arguments had no effect, they turned to threats. They told her 'that she was so unnatural to oppose the King's will so obstinately, that they could scarcely believe that she was his bastard, and if she were their daughter, they would beat her and knock her head so violently against the wall that they would make it as soft as baked apples, and that she was a traitor and should be punished'. But Mary still refused to sign.

Mary was now in great danger. When the King heard that she had refused to sign the articles, his first reaction was to order that she should be arrested and sent to the Tower; but the Privy Council, realising that this would almost inevitably mean that she would be proceeded against and executed under the Act of Supremacy, were alarmed, and interceded for her with Henry. They pointed out the effect which such a step might have in the country, and particularly the harm which it would do to relations with the Emperor. Cranmer was one of the most active members of the Council on Mary's behalf. The Council persuaded Henry to give Mary a second chance. He agreed not to send her to the Tower, but sent Norfolk and the Privy Councillors back to her to require her once again to sign the articles. He ordered the Privy Councillors to arrest Lady Hussey, who was in charge of Mary's household, and question her thoroughly to see if she was responsible for Mary's attitude. According to Chapuys, he even talked about arresting Cromwell. He was furious with Cromwell for having tried to help Mary.

Cromwell wrote to Mary and urged her to sign the articles at once. 'Knowing how diversely and contrarily you have proceeded at the late being of His Majesty's Council with you', he wrote, 'I am ashamed of what I have said and afraid of what I have done. What the sequel shall be, God knows. ... To be plain with you, I think you the most obstinate woman that ever was.' Chapuys also strongly urged her to submit and sign the articles. He wrote to her secretly and told her that to save her life 'she must dissemble for some time', as the protests which she had made, and the cruel violence shown her, would safeguard her conscience, as 'God regardeth more the intention than the act.'

64

At eleven o'clock at night on Thursday 15 June 1536, Mary decided to submit; but to judge from the form of the document which she signed, she made a last desperate attempt to avoid impugning her mother's cause and honour. She admitted that she had gravely offended Henry, and asked him for his 'mercy and fatherly pity, desiring no state, no condition, nor no manner degree of living but such as your Grace shall appoint unto me, knowing and confessing that my state cannot be so vile as either the extremity of justice would appoint unto me, or as mine offences have required and deserved'. She declared that she accepted Henry as Supreme Head of the Church of England, and rejected 'the Bishop of Rome's pretended authority'. Then she signed her name, 'Marye', without having referred to her mother's divorce.

She was not allowed to get away with this. The Privy Councillors spotted the omission, and she had to add a post-script, in which she declared 'that the marriage heretofore had between His Majesty and my mother, the late Princess Dowager, was, by God's law and man's law, incestuous and unlawful'.

By this painful humiliation, Mary had won her father's forgiveness. Six months later she came to Court at Greenwich, for Christmas, where she was received with every mark of kindness by the King and Queen Jane Seymour. Mary was only twenty, but her experiences had turned her into an able and cunning politician. Henry, with his typical hypocrisy and self-deception, asked her whether she was sincere in signing the articles and in her repentance for her past errors, and said that he hoped that she was not dissimulating, because he hated dissimulators. Mary assured him that she was completely sincere and was not dissimulating. But she wrote secretly to the Emperor and told him that she had only signed the articles under duress. She asked Charles to obtain a secret dispensation from the Pope, which would permit her to break her word and repudiate the articles, as she had not the slightest intention of keeping them any longer than was necessary.

3 The Return

to Court 1537-47

ON 12 OCTOBER 1537 Jane Seymour gave birth to a son, who afterwards became King Edward VI. Mary was his godmother at his christening and confirmation at Hampton Court; the Duke of Norfolk and Cranmer were his godfathers at the font, and the Duke of Suffolk was godfather at the bishopping. After the ceremony, Mary and the highest ranks of the nobility were served with spices and hypocras, the sweet liqueur which was always served at the grandest functions in the sixteenth century, while the lesser nobles and the gentry were given bread and sweet wine. They then left the chapel, with Mary walking in the procession side by side with her sister Elizabeth, who was just four. At last Henry had a legitimate son, who was recognised as legitimate by Protestants and Catholics in every country in Europe. Mary willingly recognised that her new brother took precedence over her as the lawful heir to the crown, and as he grew up she became very fond of him.

Twelve days after Edward was born, Jane Seymour died of post-natal complications. On 12 November her corpse was carried in great state from Hampton Court to Windsor, where it was buried with the full ceremonies of the Catholic religion, which were still used in England. All the great dignitaries of the realm rode in the funeral cortège. Mary, as chief mourner, rode immediately behind the corpse, on a horse draped with black velvet, and took a leading part in the funeral at Windsor.

As soon as Jane died, Henry began to think of marrying for the fourth time, and considered various European princesses as possible brides. At the same time, he renewed his efforts to marry Mary, who was now aged twenty-one, to a suitable foreign prince. Francis I had not forgotten about Mary, and even during the time when she was in disgrace, before the fall of Anne Boleyn, he had suggested that she should marry either his eldest son, Francis the Dauphin, or his third son, Charles, Duke of Angoulême. Charles V, who as usual was at war with France, with great generosity did not oppose the projected match, out of regard for Mary's interests. He thought that if Mary married the Dauphin or the Duke of Angoulême, Henry would have to recognise her as legitimate, and it would enable her to escape from her father's power. Although the Dauphin had never met Mary, he persuaded himself that he was madly in love with her, on the strength of the ambassadors' reports of her beauty and qualities, or perhaps from a romantic idea that this was the appropriate attitude for a young prince to adopt. He told his aunt, Queen Margaret of Navarre, that he would give one of his hands to have Mary. The Duke of Angoulême was as much in love with her as his brother, though he, too, had never met her. But Henry would not provide a suitable dowry for Mary.

In 1538 there was a prospect of another excellent match for Mary, when Dom Luiz, the brother of the King of Portugal, was a suitor for her hand; but again the negotiations broke down because of disagreements about the dowry. There was also the difficulty that Mary was regarded as illegitimate under English law, because Charles v was wrong when he thought that Henry would be forced to recognise Mary as legitimate if he wished to marry her to a foreign prince. Cromwell sent instructions to the English ambassadors abroad that they were to explore the possibilities of arranging a suitable match for Mary, emphasising to potential foreign suitors that she was beautiful, gifted and virtuous, although she was 'His Grace's daughter natural only'.

This made it difficult for foreign sovereigns to accept her as a bride for their sons without loss of prestige; and the fact that they themselves, as loyal supporters of the Pope in his dispute with Henry, regarded Mary as legitimate, only increased the difficulties from a diplomatic point of view.

In 1539 Mary was confronted with a new danger. Henry opened negotiations for an alliance with the Lutheran princes of Germany. He married Anne of Cleves, the sister of the young Duke of Jülich and Cleves, and at the same time considered marrying Mary to a German Protestant prince. This prospect filled Mary with horror. If she went to live in Germany as the wife of a German Lutheran ruler, she would have to adopt her husband's religion. She said that she would rather die an old maid than marry a Protestant.

Henry and Cromwell went ahead with their plans without paying any attention to Mary's protests. The first suitor whom they considered was the Duke of Jülich and Cleves, Anne's brother; then they thought of a better match, and proposed Duke Philip of Bavaria. When this leading Protestant prince came to England in 1539 to negotiate the marriage between

An ivory box and lid containing the portrait of Anne of Cleves, Henry's fourth wife. Henry was greatly impressed by her picture but revolted by her when they met face to face.

Henry and Anne of Cleves, he was introduced to Mary at Enfield; and a few months later, a draft treaty was drawn up, by which Mary was to marry Philip and renounce all claims to the English throne.

Fortunately for Mary, a change in Henry's policy brought these negotiations to a halt. When Henry saw Anne of Cleves, he had a great sexual aversion to her, and within six months he had made Convocation annul his marriage to Anne on the grounds of his inability to consummate the marriage. At the same time he arrested Cromwell and beheaded him; and to show that he would not tolerate any opposition from either Protestant heretics or Papist traitors, he had three Protestants burned and three papal supporters hanged, drawn and quartered on the same day at Tyburn, after all six had been dragged through the streets of London to the place of execution on hurdles, with one papal supporter and one Protestant tied together on each hurdle. One of the three Catholic martyrs was Mary's old tutor, Featherston; another was Abel, who had been Catherine of Aragon's confessor. Each one of the six went to his death sincerely believing that he was a martyr for God's truth, and that his fellow-victim beside him on the hurdle was being most justly punished for his heresy or treason.

70

After the fall of Cromwell in 1540, Henry VIII pursued a much more Catholic policy. During the last six years of his reign, nineteen Protestants were burned and many more imprisoned, while on only one occasion were three men arrested and executed for upholding papal supremacy. Henry's pro-Catholic policy was strengthened in 1543 when Charles V made an alliance with him, and England and the Empire together waged war against France, Scotland and the German Lutheran princes. Charles V, whose wife had died, offered to marry Mary, nearly twenty years after he had broken off his engagement to her; but again Henry would not agree about the dowry.

Mary herself was not at all unhappy that her marriage prospects were receding, because she had developed a great aversion to the idea of sex. She had acquired from her mother, and her mother's Spanish ladies, the teachings of the medieval Catholic theologians who condemned sex as something sinful, and thought that chastity alone was a worthy moral state. Mary, unlike most Christian princes and princesses, took these doctrines very seriously. Her youthful experiences of her father's matrimonial and sexual adventures had not made her look favourably on the idea of marriage and love. The difficulties about dowry and politics repeatedly prevented her from marrying, and in effect forced her to live a chaste life whether she wished to or not; because, even if she had wanted to have a love affair, and had not been prevented by her religious scruples, she knew that if she had an affair, and was found out, both she and her lover would be put to death for high treason. Apart from everything else, it was almost a psychological necessity for Mary to develop her dislike of sex, if her life at Henry's Court was to be bearable.

In October 1541, while the negotiations for Mary's marriage to the Duke of Orleans were in progress, the French Ambassador in London, Marillac, wrote a very full and frank description of Mary for Francis I. He had been instructed to write honestly, and to give precise information about her physical features, so that Francis could judge how suitable she would be for the purpose of bearing children. Marillac reported that the Lady Mary was of medium height, with big bones and no surplus fat. Her face, and particularly her mouth, were very like those of the King her father, and so were her laugh and her tone of voice.

Mary's voice was not quite as masculine as these words of Marillac's suggest, because Henry VIII had a very high-pitched and almost treble voice; but Marillac stated that Mary had a more masculine voice for a woman than Henry had for a man. 'Her beauty, Sire, is mediocre', he wrote, 'and I cannot say that she is one of the beautiful women at this Court.' She was very athletic and energetic; whenever the weather was fine, she walked two or three miles in the park in the morning, and when she was indoors she was more often walking around the room than sitting down. Marillac described her accomplishments, her perfect mastery of French and Latin in both writing and speaking, and her skill with the spinet and other musical instruments. Her health occasionally caused some anxiety, as she sometimes had palpitations of the heart; but a woman of her bedchamber, who had married a Frenchman and knew Marillac, told him that she had no reason to believe that Mary would be incapable of bearing healthy children.

In 1543 Henry announced that he had 'deigned to marry' his sixth wife, Katherine Parr, the widow of Lord Latimer. She was an intellectual, and interested in theology, and was sympathetic to Protestant doctrines. But despite her religious views, she and Mary became close friends. They not only did embroidery together, and played to each other on the spinet, but also read together Erasmus's *Paraphrases of the New Testament*. Mary translated Erasmus's book into English, and at Katherine's suggestion allowed her translation to be published. It would be interesting to know whether Mary really appreciated what she was doing in translating Erasmus's *Paraphrases*. When they were first published thirty years before, they had been strongly condemned as an encouragement to heresy by the Pope and the Catholic Church, although since that date Erasmus had become more orthodox, chiefly because of his fear of the anti-intellectual elements in German Lutheranism, and of the threat to cosmopolitan culture which might follow a breakdown of the authority of the international Church.

In February 1544 the Duke of Nájera, who was one of the leading noblemen in Spain, visited the English Court. His secretary, Pedro de Gente, who accompanied him, wrote a most enthusiastic description of Mary. At a great ball given in Nájera's honour, Mary appeared wearing a petticoat of

OPPOSITE Katherine Parr, Henry's last wife, who briefly was able to make some sort of home life for Henry's three children.

72

KATHARINE PARRE

Tudor Music

Music-making was a popular entertainment among all levels of society in Tudor times. It was an accomplishment that every gentleman had to acquire and a recreation among the common people. Every court and many nobles kept a permanent band of professional musicians while groups of villagers provided music in the parish churches.

BELOW A wind-band and choir in church.

RIGHT The personification of music from a woodcut in the *Margarit Philosophica* of the early sixteenth century.

OPPOSITE Orlando di Lesso and his musicians playing before the Duke of Bavaria.

74

An allegorical picture
showing a bed–ridden
Henry VIII indicating his
Protestant son, Edward,
as his successor, and thus
confounding the Pope.

cloth-of-gold, a violet-coloured gown of three-piled velvet, and a headdress with many rich stones. Nájera and his secretary thought that she danced most graciously; and when the Duke, after kissing Queen Katherine Parr's hand, offered to kiss Mary's hand, she would not permit it, and instead offered him her cheek to kiss, which was the recognised mode of greeting among equals. Gente was impressed not only with her intellectual accomplishments but also with her modesty, which seemed to him to prove that she was indeed a learned woman, because he thought that really learned people were usually modest, while those with only a little learning tended to boast about it. Mary's only critic, at this time, was her precocious and rather priggish brother, Edward. In May 1546, when he was aged eight and a half, he wrote to Katherine Parr and suggested that she should tell Mary 'to attend no longer to foreign dances and merriments, which do not become a most Christian Princess'.

In 1544 Parliament passed an Act to deal with the difficulties which had arisen about the succession to the crown. Prince Edward was recognised by everyone as the lawful heir; but he was only six, and if he died before he married and had a child, this would leave Mary and Elizabeth, both of whom had been declared illegitimate by Act of Parliament. The next in line was Mary Queen of Scots, who was thirteen months old, and was the grand-daughter of Henry VIII's sister Margaret, the wife of James IV of Scotland; but this raised difficulties, especially at the moment, when England and Scotland were at war. After her came Margaret Douglas, Countess of Lennox, the daughter of Queen Margaret by her second husband, the Earl of Angus, whom Queen Margaret had married after the death of James IV. Next were Lady Frances Brandon and her daughters, Lady Jane and Lady Katherine Grey, who were the daughter and grand-daughters of Henry VIII's other sister, Mary, who had married King Louis XII of France as her first husband, and after his death, as her second husband, Charles Brandon, Duke of Suffolk. Parliament decided to solve these complications by passing an Act which gave Henry a power, which no previous King of England had had, of bequeathing the crown of England by his Will.

At Christmas 1546 Henry made his Will, in which he directed that the crown should go, first, to Edward and his heirs; next, to Mary and her heirs, subject to the condition that she did not marry without the consent of the Privy Council; next, to Elizabeth and her heirs, subject to the same condition; and then to the children of Frances Brandon. A month later, on a bitterly cold night at the end of January 1547, Henry died.

4 The Protestant King 1547-53

EDWARD VI WAS NINE when he became King, and the power passed to his uncle, Edward Seymour, Jane Seymour's brother, who was now created Duke of Somerset, and became Lord Protector for the young King. Somerset and Archbishop Cranmer set out to make England a Protestant country. In the first two years of Edward's reign they introduced, slowly and cautiously, a number of Protestant reforms into the doctrine and practice of the Church of England. These new doctrines and practices, which a man would have been burned for advocating in Henry's reign, were now enforced by law. The heresy statute of 1401, under which Protestants had been burned, and other statutes against heresy which had been passed under Henry VIII, were repealed; and though Somerset and the Council punished any Catholic who opposed the new Protestant reforms, and any Protestants who tried to move too far and too fast in a more Protestant direction, the offenders were not burned, or executed. At the worst they were imprisoned indefinitely, without trial, in a sort of preventive detention; but in most cases they were released after a scolding and a warning from the Privy Council.

The opposition to the religious policy of Somerset and Cranmer was led by Gardiner. It was not easy for Gardiner, who had so strongly supported the doctrine of royal supremacy in Henry VIII's reign, to oppose the authority of the King's government now that it was being used to turn England into a Protestant country; but he put forward a theory that the royal absolute power over the Church could only be exercised by an adult king in person, and not by a regent on behalf of an infant king. He therefore argued that Somerset should not make any change in religion, but should leave things as they stood at Henry VIII's death, until Edward VI was old enough to decide for himself what he wished to do about religion.

Mary adopted the same attitude as Gardiner. In doing this, she was being insincere, but was showing herself to be a skilful politician. Mary did not really approve of religion as it existed at the time of Henry's death, because she still believed that the authority of the Pope should be restored over the Church of England, and that the few Protestant innovations which Henry had introduced should be done away with. She would have liked to have seen religion restored to the state in which it stood

82

Edward Seymour, Duke of
Somerset, the brother of
Jane Seymour and Lord
Protector for his nephew
Edward VI.

in 1533, not 1547. But if she had publicly taken this position, she
would have found herself politically isolated. She would also
have laid herself open to a prosecution for high treason if she
had advocated papal supremacy, for the Act of Supremacy of
Henry VIII's reign was still in force, though no one was executed
under it in Edward VI's reign. But by taking her stand in favour
of Henry VIII's religious settlement against the innovations
which Somerset and Cranmer were now introducing, Mary
could ally herself with Gardiner and his Catholic party, and
was only liable to be punished, not for high treason, but by
fines and imprisonment under the much milder laws which
were being enacted to enforce the new Protestant measures.

Although Mary was fond of her brother, the young King,
and was on friendly personal terms with Somerset, the new

84

government policy made it embarrassing for her to remain at Court, and she withdrew to her houses in the country. Henry had left her, in his Will, four houses in south-eastern England – Kenninghall in Norfolk, Newhall and Copthall in Essex, and Hunsdon in Hertfordshire. At Christmas 1547 she came to Court at Hampton Court for the usual festivities; but she did not come the following Christmas, and in the next five years only very occasionally visited her brother. For the first two years of Edward's reign she lived quietly and uneventfully, spending most of her time at Kenninghall, which was the furthest of all her manors from London and the Court.

Mary was aged thirty-two, but the government had not finally given up hope of arranging a suitable marriage for her. Dom Luiz of Portugal renewed his proposal, and the Duke of Ferrara suggested that she should marry his son. Another suitor was the German Lutheran Prince Albert of Brandenburg, Duke of Prussia, who ruled the territory that later became known as East Prussia from his capital at Königsberg. These marriage negotiations were broken off in 1549, when Mary fell ill, and were never resumed.

In the spring of 1549, Somerset and Cranmer took a step which put an end to Mary's peaceful life in the country. Cranmer had produced his Book of Common Prayer, which introduced a new communion service, in English, in place of the old Catholic Latin service of the Mass; and in December 1548 he and the Protestant bishops, for the first time, publicly declared in the House of Lords that they rejected the doctrine of transubstantiation. They would have been burned if they had said this in Henry VIII's reign. In March 1549 Parliament passed the Act of Uniformity, which enacted that the new service of the Book of Common Prayer was to be used in every church in England, and made it an offence to use any other religious service. This meant that it was henceforth to be a crime for a priest to celebrate the Catholic Mass, and for a layman to go to Mass. The punishment for the first offence was a fine of £10 – about £500 in terms of today's money; but the penalties increased for subsequent offences, and for the third offence the punishment was imprisonment for life. At the same time, Parliament passed another Act permitting one of the most controversial of all the Protestant innovations – the marriage of priests.

Under the Act of Uniformity, Mary and her chaplains were liable to be fined and imprisoned if Mass was celebrated in her household; but Charles v's Ambassador, Van der Delft, who had replaced Chapuys, asked Somerset, as a favour to the Emperor, to permit Mary to break the law and continue to hear Mass in private in her household. He also asked that he himself should be allowed to have Mass celebrated in his embassy. Somerset was still considering the matter when a series of revolts broke out in southern England. In some places, the rebels had social grievances; they objected to the enclosures of common land by local landowners which had been taking place in recent years. In other places, they revolted against the new Book of Common Prayer and the abolition of the Mass. Most of the revolts were quickly suppressed; but in Devon and Cornwall, and in Norfolk, the risings were much more formidable. The western men demanded the restoration of the Mass and the re-enactment of the heresy laws under which Protestant heretics could be burned. The rebellion in Norfolk, which was led by Kett, was concerned only with social and economic grievances. The Norfolk rebels, in so far as they had any strong religious views, tended to be extreme Protestants, with vaguely nonconformist and egalitarian doctrines about the problems of State and Church.

Somerset, finding himself with two serious rebellions on his hands, was perhaps more eager than he might otherwise have been to placate the Emperor. He promised Van der Delft that he could have Mass celebrated in his embassy, and that Mary could do the same in her houses in private.

Somerset and the Council were worried about Mary's position at Kenninghall, which was in an area controlled by the Norfolk rebels, and was only twenty miles from Kett's head-quarters at Norwich. But Mary was careful not to make any gesture which could be interpreted as an encouragement to rebellion. She would have been more tempted to do so if she had been living in the district of the Catholic rebellion in Devon and Cornwall, because she had no sympathy with the social and economic grievances of the Norfolk rebels, and disapproved of their objects as much as did the other members of the landowning classes.

The government assembled an army of German, Italian and

Spanish mercenaries, and by the end of August had crushed both the western men and Kett. Six weeks later, John Dudley, Earl of Warwick, who had defeated Kett, carried through a *coup d'état* against Somerset. Somerset had shown some sympathy with the social grievances of the people, and was blamed by the nobility and the landowners for having encouraged the rebellions by his weakness. He was sent to the Tower; and although he was released from prison next year and had a formal reconciliation with Warwick, he was executed on a trumped-up charge of treason in 1552.

Woodcuts showing
the chief events of
Edward's reign.

The Coronation of King Edward the Sixt

Popery banished True Religion Restor'd~

The D. of Somerset L. Protector Beheade

John Dudley, Earl of Warwick, who became the Duke of Northumberland after his successful *coup d'etat* against Somerset. His determination to retain power after Edward's death led to the temporary elevation into a puppet queen of the unlucky Lady Jane Grey.

Mary was as cautious during Warwick's *coup d'état* of October 1549 as she had been a few months earlier during the rebellions in the summer. During the week when the success of the *coup d'état* was in doubt, she gave no sign of support for either side. For a few weeks after the success of the *coup* the Catholics hoped, and the Protestants feared, that the new government would reverse Somerset's religious policy; but Warwick, who became Duke of Northumberland in 1551, decided to pursue a more

A caricature of c 1550 on the rapidly changing fashions of Tudor England. It shows a man holding shears and a roll of cloth, wondering what he will wear next.

extreme Protestant policy than Somerset had done. He was influenced chiefly by preachers like John Hooper and the Scottish refugee John Knox, who advocated doctrines which were too Protestant for Cranmer and many of the Protestant bishops. Northumberland may have had some sincere religious beliefs, but he was widely suspected of using Protestantism as an excuse for personal enrichment, because he took for himself and his friends a large part of the proceeds of the sale of the shrines, chantries, altar cloths and ecclesiastical vestments which were suppressed and seized at the demand of the Protestant enthusiasts who supported him.

As England, under Northumberland, became more Protestant, Mary became alarmed. She told Van der Delft that she hoped that the Emperor would quickly arrange for her to be married to Dom Luiz of Portugal; but that if this could not be done, she wished in any case to escape from England, where she feared for her safety if she continued to remain true to the Catholic faith. The Ambassador realised the difficulties about arranging for her to escape. Apart from the big risk that the attempt would fail, and that Mary would then be in much greater danger than before, if it succeeded it would not only strain relations between England and the Empire, but would make it impossible for Mary to succeed to the throne if Edward died without heirs. But Mary thought that if Edward died, she would immediately be put to death by the Protestants. She wanted only to be able to go to some country where she could lead a Christian life in peace, by which she meant that she would be allowed to attend Mass; and she was so insistent that Van der Delft agreed to refer the matter to Charles v. Charles authorised Van der Delft to arrange the escape.

Van der Delft then worked out a plan. He was to be recalled from England in order to be replaced by a new ambassador, and after leaving London, his ship was to call at Maldon in Essex, which was only three miles from the house at Woodham Walter where Mary was staying. He was to pick up Mary at Maldon, and sail with her to the Netherlands. This would have the advantage that Van der Delft himself would leave England with her, and escape from the wrath of the English government when they found out how he had exceeded his diplomatic privileges.

Van der Delft sent his secretary, Jean Dubois, to visit Mary in secret and discuss the plan with her. All the arrangements were made, and Van der Delft duly presented his letters of recall from the Emperor; but at the last moment the scheme had to be abandoned. The local authorities in Essex, having heard a false report that a new peasant rising was about to break out in the district, roused the watch, and placed constables to guard the roads near Maldon. It was clear that, in view of this, it would be very difficult for Mary to go from Woodham Walter to Maldon without being seen and recognised. So Dubois suggested an alternative plan, to which Mary agreed. After Van der Delft and Dubois had left England, Dubois was to return, disguised as a sea-captain in command of a merchant ship which was ostensibly bringing corn from the Netherlands to Maldon. He would be escorted by the Emperor's Admiral, d'Eecke, with eight imperial warships. D'Eecke would wait off the Essex coast, pretending to be operating against Scottish pirates, while Dubois sailed up the Blackwater River to Maldon with his corn. While Dubois, in Maldon, was negotiating the sale of his corn, Mary would come there from Woodham Walter. She would then sail down the Blackwater in Dubois's ship to the open sea, where she would go on board d'Eecke's flagship and be carried to Antwerp.

Dubois arrived at Maldon with his corn at 2 a.m. on Wednesday 2 July 1550. A few hours later he met Robert Rochester, the Controller of Mary's household, who came in disguise to a prearranged spot in the churchyard of St Mary's Church in Maldon. Rochester took Dubois to the house of a trustworthy friend in Maldon, where they could talk freely; but he then told Dubois that Mary was not sure that she wished to go through with the plan, because if she left England she would forfeit her right to the crown. Dubois said that he and Van der Delft were well aware of this, and had pointed it out to Mary, but that Mary had nevertheless insisted on going, and that it was a little late to raise this objection now. He refused to abandon the attempt unless Mary herself told him to do so. While Dubois's officers negotiated with a merchant in Maldon about the sale of the corn, and tried to spin out the negotiations for as long as possible, Rochester led Dubois to Woodham Walter by a path through the woods, without anyone seeing them; and Dubois spent the afternoon discussing the matter with Mary.

Rochester strongly urged Mary not to go. He said that the astrologers had foretold that Edward VI would die within a year, and that if Mary was in England when he died, she would succeed to the crown. Mary herself could not make up her mind. She told Dubois that she wished to go, but that she had not yet packed her belongings, and asked Dubois to postpone their departure for forty-eight hours until Friday. Dubois said that if she reached the Netherlands the Emperor would provide her with everything that she could possibly need, and that it would be very dangerous for him and his men to wait another two days at Maldon, as they would have no excuse to do so after the corn had been sold; and suspicions might be aroused by the presence of his ship at Maldon or by d'Eecke's warships off the coast. He advised Mary that if she wanted to escape, the attempt should be made that night.

Mary was still hesitating when Rochester came in and told them that d'Eecke's warships had been sighted, and that the local authorities, realising that something was afoot, had alerted the whole neighbourhood. A man had been stationed in the tower of St Mary's Church in Maldon to watch out for any movements in the district, and they were preparing to light the beacons in the area to warn everyone to be on their guard against the enemy. It was therefore decided that Dubois should leave at once, without Mary; and after making tentative arrangements for another escape attempt to be made in the near future, Dubois left Mary, who was in great distress, and kept repeating 'What will become of me?'

When Dubois got back to Maldon, he saw no sign of a man in the church tower or of any other precautions being taken by the authorities, and he thought that Rochester had invented the story in order to prevent Mary from going; but he sailed away, and rejoined d'Eecke, with whom he returned to the Netherlands. The plans for Mary's escape were then cancelled on the Emperor's orders. If it had not been for Rochester, Mary would probably have escaped, and would never have come to the throne; the lives of the Protestant martyrs, and Mary's historical reputation, would have been saved; and many future generations of English Catholics might have been spared much persecution and victimisation.

As Mary had feared, she was soon in difficulties about her Mass. The Duke of Northumberland's government did not consider themselves bound by the promise which Somerset had given to the Emperor's ambassador, and tried to prevent Mary from having Mass celebrated in her household. They objected because she often permitted Catholic residents in the neighbourhood to be present at her Mass, which was an abuse of the privilege which had been granted to her alone; and they arrested her chaplain, Francis Mallet, because on one occasion, when Mary had been absent from the house, he had held Mass for the other members of her household. The matter was taken up by the young King himself. Edward was only twelve, but was a very intelligent child, and had adopted Protestant doctrines with a boy's enthusiasm. From 1550 onwards, he wrote letters to Mary, urging her to see the error of her ways, to abandon her Mass and to conform, like all his other subjects, to the new service of the Book of Common Prayer. He would not accept the argument that the King's power could not be exercised during his infancy. 'Dear and well-beloved sister', he wrote, 'we hold ourselves to possess the same authority our father had for the administration of the republic. The Scriptures abound in instances to prove that the best ordered Church of the people of Israel was instituted and upheld by Kings younger in years than we.' Mary treated these letters as having been written in the King's name by Protestant Councillors who were unscrupulously using the royal authority of her dear brother for their heretical purposes; but though these letters of Edward's were undoubtedly drafted by, or with the assistance of, the King's secretaries and ministers, the private diary which Edward kept from the age of eleven onwards shows that he himself completely agreed with the Protestant opinions which were expressed in the letters.

At Christmas 1550 the Council summoned Mary to come to Court at Greenwich. When she arrived, Edward kissed her tenderly, but then proceeded to upbraid her, in public before all the courtiers, for attending Mass in her houses. Mary burst into tears.

Three months later, Mary was again summoned to Court. She travelled from Newhall to Westminster in great state, riding through London, by Cheapside and Smithfield, with fifty knights and gentlemen going in front, and eighty ladies and gentlemen behind. They all of them ostentatiously carried the beads of their rosaries, which had been condemned as superstitious by the Protestants. There were great demonstrations in Mary's favour all along the road, where crowds had gathered to see her pass. When she reached Whitehall, the Council ordered her to obey the Act of Uniformity and cease having

Mass celebrated in her houses; but the Emperor's new ambassador, Scheyvfe, intervened strongly on her behalf.

Scheyvfe and Charles v felt able to adopt a much higher tone towards Edward vi's ministers than they would have dared to assume if Henry viii, or any adult King, had been reigning in Emperor to place an embargo on the export of the gunpowder. 'The Emperor's Ambassador came with short message from his master of war if I would not suffer his cousin the Princess to use her Mass.' Scheyvfe was bluffing, but the English government could not be sure of this. In any case, they had ordered a large consignment of gunpowder which was at Antwerp, waiting to be shipped to England; and they did not want the Emperor to place an embargo on the export of gunpowder. They therefore decided to give way, and promised Scheyvfe that Mary would be allowed to continue to hold Mass in her house.

They ran into an unexpected difficulty. The twelve-year-old

Edward vi and his Council, from a woodcut on the title to the Acts of Parliament, 1551.

95

King was indignant at their decision. He told his Council that his tutors had taught him that it was a sin to license sin, and that he would therefore be committing a sin if he allowed Mary to commit the sin of attending a Catholic Mass. The Council sent three of the most eminent Protestant bishops – Archbishop Cranmer, Nicholas Ridley, Bishop of London, and John Ponet, Bishop of Rochester – to persuade the King to give way. They told him that though it was indeed a sin to license sin, yet the sin of the Mass might be 'winked at' for a short time if the overriding interests of the realm required it. Edward accepted this argument with some misgivings.

Mary had gained a breathing-space, but the Council did not intend to wink at her Mass indefinitely. They resented the Emperor's attitude, because, while he insisted that his ambassador in London should be allowed to have Mass in his house, he refused to allow the English ambassador at his Court to hold the Protestant service of the Book of Common Prayer in the English embassy. The English government sent Nicholas Wotton, who was Dean of both Canterbury and York, to visit Charles v at Augsburg in Bavaria to thrash out the difficulties. This meant a respite of several months for Mary, while Wotton travelled to Augsburg and back and discussed the matter with Charles.

Charles had a long discussion with Wotton, but he would not change his attitude. He said that under no circumstances whatever would he allow a foreign ambassador at his Court to hold a Protestant service in the embassy. If the English government insisted on preventing his ambassador in London from holding Mass in his embassy, they were entitled to do so, but in that case he would withdraw his ambassador from London. As far as Mary was concerned, Charles used threatening language, and said that he would not permit her to be deprived of her Mass; if the worst came to the worst, Mary would be 'the first martyr of royal blood to die for our holy faith'.

The English government were incensed at Charles's attitude, especially as he had, after all, placed an embargo on the export of the gunpowder at Antwerp. They did not want to sever diplomatic relations with him, and they accepted the unequal arrangement by which Charles's ambassador was allowed to hold Mass in his house although the English ambassador at

Charles's Court could not hold a Protestant service; but they were not prepared to show any more indulgence to Mary. They were in a stronger position than they had been in four months earlier, because Charles was at war with France, and was getting into serious military difficulties in his campaign against the German Lutherans. In August 1551 they summoned Rochester and two other officials of Mary's household to appear before the Council, and ordered them to prevent Mass from being celebrated in Mary's house. Rochester and his colleagues appeared to comply with the order, but returned a week later and told the Council that Mary would not permit them to enforce it. They were thereupon arrested, and sent to the Tower. Edward VI then drafted a letter to Mary. It explained that Somerset's promise to the Emperor's ambassador had not been intended to apply for ever, but was given merely because the King had agreed to allow Mary more time to see the error which she was committing. The time had now expired, and she must henceforth obey the law, like all his other subjects; if she and her chaplains broke the law, they would be punished like anyone else. The Council sent the Lord Chancellor, Lord Rich, with two other Privy Councillors, to Copthall in Essex, where Mary was living, to deliver the King's letter to her.

On 28 August Rich arrived at Copthall with his colleagues, and had an encounter with Mary which he described in his report to the Privy Council. According to his account, Mary was defiant, and not even courteous. Mary explained the reason for this to Scheyvfe; she said that she always adopted a high and harsh tone towards the Lords of the Council and their officers, because she thought that if she behaved in a milder way they would interpret it as a sign of weakness and increase their demands upon her. She did not invite Rich and his colleagues into the house, but met them in the courtyard and talked to them there. When they handed the King's letter to her, she received it on her knees and kissed it in the proper manner; but she assumed that it had been drafted for Edward by the Secretary of State, William Cecil, who was beginning his career as a minister which he afterwards pursued so successfully for forty years under Elizabeth I. As she read Edward's letter, she commented at one point: 'Ah, good Mr Cecil took much pains here', and made other similar comments to the indignant Privy

A coin of 1551 showing
Edward VI on horseback.

Councillors. She said that she was the King's 'most humble, most obedient subject and poor sister', and would obey the King in everything, 'her conscience saved', but that, rather than adopt any service except that used at the death of Henry VIII, she would lay her head on a block and suffer death, though she was unworthy to die in so good a quarrel. When the King was old enough to judge these things himself, she would obey him in religion, 'but now, in these years, although he, good sweet King, have more knowledge than any other of his years, yet it is not possible that he can be a judge in these things'. Rich told her that the officers of her household and her chaplains would be imprisoned if Mass was said in her house. She replied that the Council could deal with her officers and priests as they thought fit, but that she did not think that her priests would be frightened by such threats, because the laws against the Mass were mild. When she came to the throne, she did not make this mistake in dealing with her Protestant opponents.

She turned her back on Rich and his colleagues, and flounced off into the house; but a few moments later, she appeared at an upstairs window, and, leaning out of it, added a few more words of defiance in a loud voice, for all her household to hear. Rich offered to come up to her if she had anything more that she wished to say to them; but she would not agree to this. She shouted to them that she hoped that the Council would soon release Rochester and send him back to her, because, since he had been in prison, she had had to learn to manage her own accounts, and 'how many loaves of bread be made of a bushel of wheat'; and 'my father and mother never brought me up with baking and brewing', and she was weary of it.

Rochester and Mary's other officers, and some of her chaplains, were held in prison for several months; but no steps were taken against Mary herself, and as she had other chaplains in her household, and they were prepared to risk imprisonment for their faith, they regularly celebrated Mass for her, in the strictest secrecy. The Council made no further effort to suppress her Mass. Officially, they acted on the assumption that Mass was no longer being celebrated in her house; but after she became Queen, Mary told the Emperor's ambassador that the Privy Council in Edward's reign knew very well that she continued all the time to attend Mass.

OVERLEAF Eight stages in breadmaking from the manual of the breadmakers of York. Beneath each picture are rhyming couplets giving sound advice. The page concludes '*Who so followeth these preceptes well In heaven shall have a place to dwell.*'

99

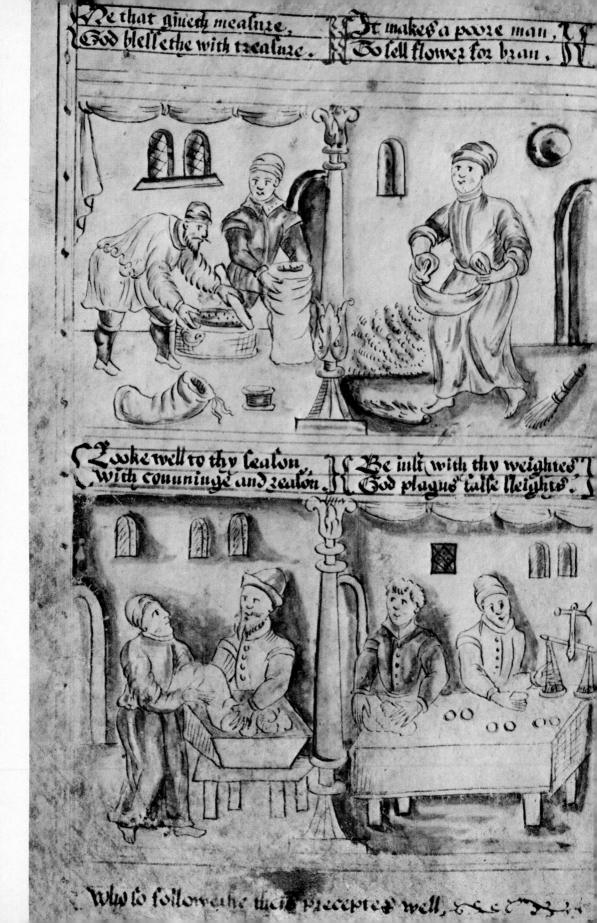

He that giueth mealuze,
God blesseth with trealuze.

It makes a poore man,
To sell flowez for bran.

Loke well to thy sealon
with cunninge and realon.

Be iust with thy weightes
God plagues false sleightes.

Wlo lo followeth their preceptes well,

God blesseth trewe laboux,
With plentye and fauour,

Be still quicke and kinde
Reward thou shalt finde

Pricke not at thy pleasure,
But in trewe honesh measure

Be watchfull and wise
In goodwille to rise :5

In heauen shall haue a place to dwell

At the beginning of September 1552, when Mary was in residence at Hunsdon, she was visited by the Bishop of London, Ridley, who was staying at his house at Hadham, three miles from Hunsdon. Ridley was perhaps the most able theologian and debater of all the Protestant bishops; it was he who had first persuaded Cranmer to reject the orthodox doctrine of the Mass and transubstantiation. Mary received him most graciously, and said that she remembered meeting him at Court during the last years of Henry VIII's reign, when Ridley had been a royal chaplain. After they had engaged for a short time in pleasant general conversation, Ridley offered to preach to her and her household on the following Sunday; but Mary told him that she would not listen to a Protestant sermon. When Ridley said that he hoped that she would not refuse to listen to God's word, she replied that what was God's word in her father's time was not God's word now; and as their argument became more heated, she said to Ridley: 'You durst not, for your ears, have avouched that for God's word in my father's days that now you do.' This was certainly true, however hypocritical it might be for Mary to take her stand in support of the religious settlement of Henry VIII. She told Ridley that she had never read a Protestant book, and would never do so; and she finally ended the interview by saying: 'My Lord, for your gentleness to come and see me, I thank you; but for your offering to preach before me, I thank you never a whit.'

In the spring of 1552, Edward VI had a dangerous attack of measles and smallpox; and, though he appeared to recover, the cure was not complete, and he gradually developed tuberculosis. By the summer of 1553 it was known at Court that he was dying. Under the Act of Parliament of 1544 and Henry VIII's Will, Mary was next in succession to the throne.

The Duke of Northumberland was determined to make a desperate attempt to preserve his power and the Protestant religion by preventing Mary from becoming Queen. In May 1553 his son Lord Guilford Dudley married Lady Jane Grey, the daughter of Frances Brandon and Henry Grey, Duke of Suffolk, and the grand-daughter of Henry VIII's sister Mary. Under Henry VIII's Will, Jane Grey was third in succession to the throne after Mary and Elizabeth. Northumberland thought that if Henry VIII could dispose of the crown of England by his

Will, Edward VI could do the same, and he proposed that Edward should make a Will bequeathing the crown to Jane Grey and cutting out Mary and Elizabeth. There was one difference in the two cases; Henry VIII had been granted power to bequeath the crown by an Act of Parliament, and Edward VI had not. Nearly all Northumberland's colleagues in the Privy Council were very doubtful of the legality of the proposal and afraid of the consequences of supporting it, especially as the Act of Parliament of 1544 had laid down that it was high treason to attempt to alter the succession as provided in the Act and in Henry VIII's Will. But Northumberland had one enthusiastic supporter – the King himself. The fifteen-year-old boy knew that he was dying, and was determined to spend his last weeks of life in ensuring that Mary did not become Queen and re-establish Popery in England.

In consultation with Northumberland, Edward drafted a Will in which he stated that he was excluding Mary and Elizabeth from the crown because they were illegitimate, and because they might marry a foreigner; and by a very complicated and far-fetched argument, he maintained that Jane Grey was the proper heir, and bequeathed the crown to her. After Edward had signed the Will, Northumberland told the Privy Council about it for the first time, and asked them to subscribe to it. They were very reluctant to agree, but were eventually persuaded to do so by Edward himself. Cranmer refused to sign unless he were first allowed to have a private audience with Edward at which Northumberland was not present. Northumberland knew that he could safely agree to this, and at their private talk Edward passionately urged and commanded Cranmer to subscribe. Cranmer then agreed to do so. On 21 June all the Privy Council subscribed to the Will.

Edward survived for only another fortnight. When it was clear that he had not long to live, Northumberland and the Council thought that they had better get Mary into their power before he died. Mary was at Hunsdon, and on 3 July she received a summons from the Council to come to Greenwich to see Edward. Her exact movements after this are uncertain. According to one account, she set off for London; but at Hoddesdon she met Sir Nicholas Throckmorton's goldsmith, who had been sent by Throckmorton to warn her that

Sawston Hall near
Cambridge where Mary
stopped on her flight.
from Northumberland's
troops.
BELOW The bedroom in
which she is traditionally
believed to have spent
the night.

Northumberland intended to arrest her. She had to take a quick and irrevocable decision. She turned back, and rode, not towards Greenwich, but to the north. She reached Sawston Hall, near Cambridge, where the owner, Mr Huddlestone, offered her his hospitality. After hearing Mass, and perhaps staying the night, at Sawston Hall, she rode on to her house at Kenninghall in Norfolk, where she arrived on 6 July. Edward VI died the same day.

The Lady Jane, Proclaimed Queen.—

Queen Mary 1553

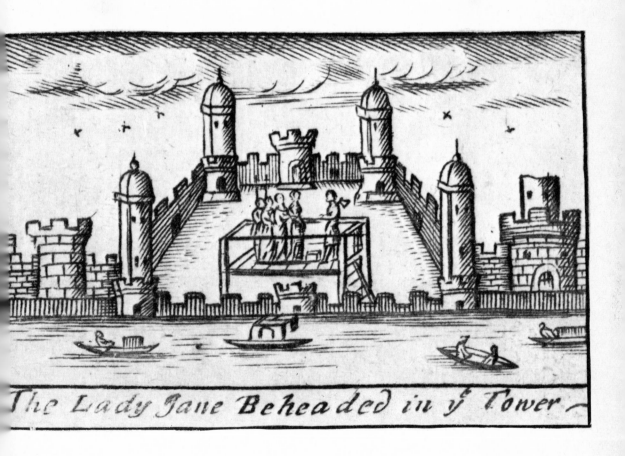

The Lady Jane Beheaded in y^e Tower

NORTHUMBERLAND AND THE COUNCIL suppressed the news of Edward VI's death for forty-eight hours. Then, on 8 July 1553, they summoned the Lord Mayor of London and the other great dignitaries of the realm, and told them that the King was dead and that Jane Grey was their lawful Queen. The Lord Mayor and all the dignitaries subscribed to Edward's grant of the crown to Jane. On 10 July Jane, who had been living at Sion House on the Thames near Isleworth, came to London by barge and took up her residence in the Tower with her husband, Lord Guilford Dudley, and her father, the Duke of Suffolk. She was proclaimed Queen in Cheapside and at the usual places in the city.

Mary, at Kenninghall, had heard the news of Edward's death by 9 July, and wrote at once to the Council in London, commanding them to recognise her as their Queen and act as her loyal subjects. They replied in a letter which informed Mary that she was a bastard and could not succeed to the crown, and called on her to show herself a loyal subject of Queen Jane. Neither side could now draw back, as either the one or the other must necessarily be guilty of high treason.

But Mary found that there was a spontaneous rising of the country gentlemen and people in her support. The Norfolk and Suffolk gentry came to Kenninghall and offered to fight for her. The gentlemen and people also rose on her behalf in Buckinghamshire and Oxfordshire, and there, as well as in Norfolk and Suffolk, she was proclaimed Queen. A few powerful nobles, like the Earl of Derby, joined her. She decided to move from Kenninghall to Framlingham Castle in Suffolk. Framlingham was easier to defend from attack than Kenninghall; and it also had the advantage of being less than fifteen miles from the coast, so that it would be easier for her to escape to the Emperor's territories if Northumberland sent troops to capture her, and the resistance of her supporters collapsed.

Northumberland and the Council hastily assembled a force of about two thousand men-at-arms and Spanish and German mercenaries in order to crush the revolt of Mary's supporters. They also ordered the fleet to go to Yarmouth and patrol the coast to stop Mary from escaping abroad.

The people of south-eastern England came out solidly for Mary. The Catholic areas of the north and west, where she

PREVIOUS PAGES The rise and fall of Lady Jane Grey illustrated in woodcuts.

might have been expected to find most support, were so far away that the people there did not find out what was happening in time to take any part in events during the decisive days. The revolution that put Mary on the throne took place in the most Protestant part of the kingdom. The Protestants afterwards claimed that they had been Mary's strongest supporters in 1553, and used this to show both their disinterested loyalty to the Crown and Mary's ingratitude towards them. Not all the people in south-eastern England who supported Mary were Protestants; but many of them were, and some of the Protestant leaders supported her. Hooper, the Protestant extremist who had been made Bishop of Worcester and Gloucester, called on his congregation to march to Framlingham and fight for Mary. Sir Peter Carew, who was an ardent Protestant, proclaimed Mary as Queen in Exeter; and John Bale, the most vitriolic

Protestant pamphleteer of the age, also supported Mary against
Jane. The only leading Protestant clerics who supported Jane
were Cranmer and Ridley, who were in Jane's capital in London,
and Edwin Sandys in Cambridge. Protestantism in England
had never, until now, been a revolutionary movement, but had
always emphasised its loyalty to the Crown; and many Protestants were glad to have the opportunity of proving this by
loyally supporting even a Catholic sovereign.

The Protestant writer John Foxe wrote in his *Book of Martyrs*
that Mary issued a proclamation at Framlingham, in which she
promised that if she became Queen she would uphold the
Protestant religion as it existed at the death of Edward VI. Foxe
states that it was on the faith of this proclamation that the
Protestants in Norfolk fought for her. But Foxe does not give
the text of the proclamation, as he does of most of the documents
to which he refers, and there is no other reference to it in any of
the many surviving contemporary records, although Charles V
advised Mary to publish a declaration on precisely these lines.
It seems quite clear that Mary never issued any such proclamation. On the other hand, the Norfolk Protestants did not
realise that they were fighting to win the crown for a Catholic
Queen who was shortly to begin a fierce persecution of
Protestants, and they seem somehow to have got hold of the
idea that Mary was not intending to restore the Catholic religion.
Probably some of her subordinate officers in Norfolk and
Suffolk, in July 1553, encouraged this idea, and Mary and her
leading advisers were careful not to enlighten her Protestant
supporters as to what her intentions really were.

There were three reasons why the people of south-eastern
England revolted in support of Mary. First, there was a feeling
among many sections of the people, even in the south-east, that
Northumberland and the Protestant bishops had been sub-
verting the true religion and introducing heresies. Secondly,
apart from the religious issue, Northumberland was very
unpopular, except among a small number of Protestant
enthusiasts, because he was believed to be a corrupt and unscrupulous politician; and there was great discontent over the
economic and social situation. The last years of Henry VIII and
the reign of Edward VI had been a period of inflation; prices,
after remaining unchanged for several centuries, had doubled

in less than ten years. The enclosures of common land by the landlords were deeply resented; and Northumberland, who had suppressed Kett's revolt and had overthrown Somerset with the support of the landowners, was hated by the peasants and labourers, particularly by the men of Norfolk who, four years before, had fought for Kett. But probably the strongest motive which led the people to fight for Mary was their sense of loyalty to the throne. The duty of the people to obey the King, not from fear of punishment in this world, but from fear of hell-fire in the next, had been proclaimed in sermons in nearly every church in the country on nearly every Sunday for the last twenty years. Whatever Edward's Will or any Act of Parliament might say, the people knew that Mary was heir to the crown by the old-established rules of hereditary succession; even though they had been told that she was illegitimate, they had seen her treated as a Princess in Edward's reign, and had been led to believe that she would become their Queen when Edward died; and none of them had expected that Jane Grey would be Queen, as they had not been given any prior notice of Edward's bequest of the crown to her.

The Emperor's ambassadors in London were watching the situation with great concern, both for Mary's safety and from the standpoint of Charles v's interests. In addition to his resident ambassador, Scheyvfe, Charles had three other representatives in London at the moment, having sent them to England a few weeks earlier to negotiate a political and commercial treaty with Edward's ministers. The ablest of these four diplomats was Simon Renard, one of Charles's French-speaking subjects from Franche-Comté, who, because of his name and his diplomatic cunning, was often nicknamed 'the fox' by his fellow-diplomats. It so happened that Charles was residing in Brussels at the moment, which made communications easier than when he was in Spain or Bavaria. His ambassadors in London could send their reports to the Emperor and receive his reply in six days.

The ambassadors told Charles that 'Suffolk's daughter' had been proclaimed Queen, that Northumberland and his supporters held London securely on her behalf, and that Mary, disobeying the summons to come to Court, had fled to Norfolk, and was asserting her right to the crown. Relying on the

Lady Jane Grey, the sixteen-year-old victim of Northumberland's plots. Her claim to the throne, through her grandmother Mary, daughter of Henry VII, was very slight and she won no popular support.

ambassadors' reports, Charles completely misjudged the situation. On 11 July he wrote to them and ordered them to advise Mary to submit to Jane, as any resistance on her part would be useless and would have fatal results for her. By the time that Renard and his colleagues received Charles's instructions, they had lost contact with Mary; and by the time that the contact had been re-established, the situation had changed so much that they took care not to tell her what Charles had written.

On 13 July, the fleet which Northumberland had sent to Yarmouth to prevent Mary from escaping abroad, mutinied, and declared for Mary. After the ships had been forced by the weather to enter port at Yarmouth, the crews contacted one of Mary's commanders, and told him that they would throw their officers into the sea if they did not join Mary. The officers then proclaimed her as Queen, and placed the fleet at her disposal. In London, broadsheets supporting Mary appeared in the streets, though the Council succeeded in suppressing the movement by severely punishing the offenders; and after a young man had been put in the pillory and had his ears cut off for supporting Mary, the opposition to Jane was driven underground. Northumberland had now assembled his soldiers and was ready to send them against Mary in Norfolk. He had to decide the difficult question as to whether to take command of them himself, or to remain in the capital. There were risks in both courses. Northumberland's first thought was to stay in London; but as all the other members of the Council insisted that he must lead the army in person, he reluctantly agreed, relying on the Duke of Suffolk to ensure that London remained loyal.

On 14 July Northumberland marched out of London at the head of his troops. As he rode through the streets, he noticed that no one cheered him, and this worried him very much. After two days' march he reached Cambridge. Here he heard that the fleet at Yarmouth had deserted to Mary, and that she had been joined by forty thousand men at Framlingham, though in fact her forces there probably numbered less than fifteen thousand men. He also noticed signs of mutiny among his own troops. The foreign mercenaries who hired themselves out as soldiers to every government who paid them did not normally concern themselves with politics, and usually served loyally as long as

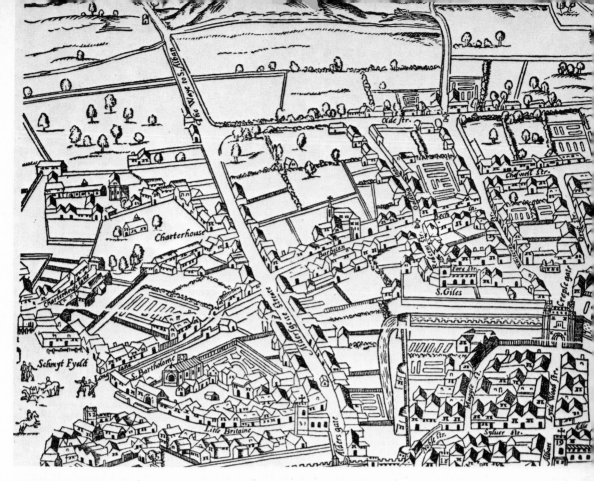

ABOVE North-east
London, showing the
suburbs extending beyond
the city wall, from the
Agas map of 1560.
LEFT A detail of Finsbury
Fields from a copperplate
of Moorfields, 1558.

their pay was not in arrears; but Northumberland's Spanish and German mercenaries had heard that Mary was a great favourite of their Emperor, and that they were fighting for the heretics against her, and they were not too happy about the position. Northumberland was so upset by all this news that he lost the ruthless resolution that he had shown in his campaigns in Scotland and against Kett, and when he carried through his *coup d'état* against Somerset. Instead of advancing against Mary at Framlingham, as he had originally intended, he waited at Cambridge for two days, and then marched to Bury St Edmunds, within thirty miles of Framlingham, only to turn round and march back to Cambridge. He probably thought that the best thing to do would be to wait until Mary's forces dispersed and went home, as usually happened in due course with rebel armies in sixteenth-century England.

In London, public opinion was secretly hardening against the government. On Sunday 16 July Ridley preached at Paul's Cross, by order of the Privy Council, and explained to the people why Jane was the lawful Queen. He declared that Mary and Elizabeth were both illegitimate, both by God's law and by Act of Parliament, and that Mary was a Papist who, if she came to the throne, intended to destroy the true religion and restore Popery; and he told his listeners how she had refused to hear him preach at Hunsdon in the previous autumn. He was shouted down by the crowd, and had to abandon his attempt to speak. That morning a paper was found fixed to the door of the church at Queenhithe, on which it was written that Mary had been proclaimed Queen everywhere except in London.

Mary's secret supporters in the Privy Council decided that the time had come to carry out a *coup d'état*. The leaders of the *coup* were Henry Fitzalan, Earl of Arundel; Francis Talbot, Earl of Shrewsbury; William Herbert, Earl of Pembroke; and William, Lord Paget. They approached all the other members of Jane's Council, except three whom they knew would be loyal to Jane – Suffolk, Cranmer and Sir John Cheke, who had been Edward VI's tutor. They managed to win over all the others without difficulty. On 19 July they visited the Lord Mayor and called on him to proclaim Mary in the city.

The news spread quickly through London, and the people came out into the streets in a spontaneous outburst of enthusiasm

OPPOSITE Mary I
by Hans Eworth.

117

Henry Fitzalan, Earl of Arundel, who turned with the tide as support for Mary grew, and lead a *coup* against Jane Grey.

which had never been seen before within living memory. Foreign observers noted with amazement, and Protestant writers remembered with bitterness for many years, this extraordinary demonstration on Wednesday 19 July 1553. When the Lord Mayor walked to the cross in Cheapside to proclaim Queen Mary, the cheering crowds in the streets were so thick that he had the greatest difficulty in getting to the cross. All the bells in the city and in Southwark were already ringing, as the priests had begun to ring them almost simultaneously in every church. People cheered, sang and danced in the streets, and it was thought that hardly anyone in London remained indoors.

The city authorities hurriedly arranged for the fountains in the streets to run with wine. When night came, bonfires were lit in the streets, and the singing, dancing and drinking went on all night. An Italian visitor wrote home that the whole city shone with lights like Mount Etna. London did not get back to normal for more than twenty-four hours, and the church bells went on ringing all next day. In the Tower, Queen Jane and Suffolk had watched, powerless and stupefied. On the afternoon of the 19th, Suffolk came into his daughter's room and told her to take down her canopy of state because her reign was over. He then went out to Tower Hill, and proclaimed Mary as Queen.

On the night of 19 July the Privy Council met, and wrote a letter to Northumberland in Cambridge, telling him what they had done, and ordering him to submit at once to his Sovereign Lady Queen Mary. The Council's messenger reached Cambridge by the afternoon of the next day. But Northumberland had already heard the news of the events in London, and an hour before the messenger from the Council arrived, he had gone out into the market place in Cambridge and proclaimed Queen Mary. Next day Arundel arrived. The Council had sent him to Framlingham to offer their submission to Mary, and she had ordered him to go to Cambridge and arrest Northumberland on a charge of high treason. Northumberland made no attempt at resistance. When he said to Arundel that he trusted that Queen Mary would show him mercy, Arundel replied that Northumberland should have thought of this before. Arundel himself had only thought of it forty-eight hours earlier; but these forty-eight hours made a great difference.

Meanwhile all the leading nobles and officials in the kingdom, particularly those who had been most active in supporting Jane, were hurrying to Framlingham to see Mary, to proclaim their allegiance to her, and to implore her pardon. She received nearly all of them, and pardoned them. Only a small number of Jane's supporters were refused admission to her presence, and were arrested. Apart from Northumberland, these included his five sons, one of whom, Lord Robert Dudley, became Earl of Leicester in Elizabeth's reign and her great favourite; Sir John Gates and Sir Thomas Palmer, two gentlemen who had been Northumberland's closest advisers; and Bishop Ridley, because of the sermon which he had preached at Paul's Cross. Jane Grey

119

Henry Grey, Duke of Suffolk, who on 19 July told his daughter Jane (opposite) that her nine days' reign was over.

and her husband, and her father Suffolk, were arrested and held in the Tower – no longer in the state apartments, but in the prisons.

Mary had triumphed. No English sovereign had ever been so popular on coming to the throne as Mary was in July 1553. She succeeded in losing most of this popularity in the course of the next five years.

6 The Spanish

Marriage 1553-4

ON 24 JULY MARY BROKE UP HER CAMP at Framlingham, and set out for London with a small body of troops. She travelled slowly, staying in her houses in Essex on the way, and receiving the homage of the local gentry wherever she passed. On 2 August she reached Wanstead, where she was met by her sister Elizabeth, who had stayed quietly at her house at Hatfield since King Edward's death, without making any move one way or the other during the ten days' reign of Queen Jane. Elizabeth now knelt to Mary as her Queen, and was most graciously received by her. Next day Mary rode to Whitechapel, and after changing her dress in a house in the village, entered London through Aldgate, with Elizabeth and all her escort accompanying her. She was greeted by cheering crowds, though five thousand countrymen, who had followed her from the Essex villages, were disappointed that they were not allowed to enter London with her, as the authorities feared that this would cause congestion and confusion in the city. As she passed the Tower, four prisoners were kneeling at the great gate to ask her royal pardon. They were not Jane Grey and any of the new inmates of the prisons, but four who had been imprisoned there for all or part of Edward VI's reign – Gardiner; the old Duke of Norfolk; the Duchess of Somerset, the widow of the former Lord Protector; and Edward Courtenay, the great-grandson of Edward IV, who had been a prisoner in the Tower ever since the age of twelve, when his father, the Marquis of Exeter, had been executed as a Papist traitor by Henry VIII in 1538. Mary looked at them and said, in a tone of shocked surprise: 'These are my prisoners!', and ordered their immediate release; and then and there, as Gardiner knelt to implore her royal pardon, she appointed him to be a member of her Privy Council. Three weeks later she appointed him Lord Chancellor. He was her chief adviser until his death two years later.

Mary took up her residence in the Tower, and stayed there for a fortnight before moving to Richmond in the middle of August. It had become an established tradition that a new sovereign lived in the Tower for a few weeks before his coronation, and then never resided there again for the rest of his reign. In the Tower, Mary turned her attention to three problems confronting her – the punishment of the traitors; the religious settlement; and the question of her marriage.

124

The Emperor's ambassadors had wasted no time in raising these matters with Mary. They had visited her at Newhall, when she was on her way to London, and had conveyed the Emperor's advice to her. As soon as Charles v heard that Mary had rejected his earlier advice and had resisted Jane, and had won, he hailed this unexpected development as an act of Providence, and determined to make the most of this wonderful opportunity. His long friendship with Mary and his attempts to protect her for twenty years now seemed likely to receive their reward. If he could rely on Mary's friendship and develop, not merely a temporary alliance with England, but a permanent and closer unity, this would transform the whole balance of power in Europe in his favour and to the detriment of France. With England holding both Dover and Calais, he could control the Channel, which was vital to him as a sea-route along which his treasure-ships brought the silver from the mines of Mexico and Peru to the money market at Antwerp. It also meant that he could almost encircle France in war-time. King Henry ii of France was as conscious of the danger as Charles was of his opportunity. Knowing Mary's friendship for the Emperor, Henry ii was very suspicious of her; and although he was busily engaged in burning and torturing his own Protestants in France with exceptional savagery, he told his ambassador in London to give secret encouragement to Mary's opponents among the English Protestants, just as he had already for some years been helping the German Lutheran princes who were fighting against Charles v.

The Emperor, in view of the great importance of England to his foreign policy, thought that London was now a post for one of his ablest diplomats, and recalling Scheyvfe and the other envoys, he left Renard there as his resident ambassador. Thanks to Renard's skill and tact, and Mary's gratitude to Charles, the Emperor's ambassador became the most influential man in England, though England under Mary was never at any time a satellite of the Emperor's, and Renard was not always able to persuade Mary to follow his advice.

Charles proposed to Mary that she should marry his son, Prince Philip of Spain. Philip was aged twenty-six, more than eleven years younger than Mary. His first wife had died, leaving him a son, Don Carlos, so he was free to marry again. Charles ordered

Edward Courtenay, Earl
of Devon, was one of
the prisoners freed on
Mary's accession. He had
been imprisoned in the
Tower since he was
a boy of eleven.

Renard to press Mary to marry Philip. Renard was also to urge
her to be ruthless in punishing the traitors, and in executing
anyone who was likely to be a political danger to her in the
future; and he was to try to restrain her religious enthusiasm,
and to persuade her to proceed very cautiously about restoring
the Catholic religion and persecuting Protestants. Renard did
not find it easy to persuade her to follow Charles's wishes on
any of these points. Her dislike of sex made her very reluctant
to marry. Her high principles and lack of personal vindictive-
ness made it difficult for her to adopt a Machiavellian approach
and find excuses for executing her political opponents and rivals
on trumped-up charges; and her religious fanaticism made her

127

eager to restore the true faith and stamp out heresy without any regard for the consequences.

Renard told her that she ought certainly to put to death Jane Grey, Guilford Dudley, Suffolk and Northumberland, and some of the prominent Lords of the Council who had supported Jane. He also suggested that it would be advisable to find an excuse to have Elizabeth arrested, as she was certain always to be a potential danger to Mary and a rallying point for Protestant and other rebels. Mary would not agree to imprison Elizabeth; and she staggered Renard by refusing even to have Jane Grey beheaded, though he warned her that if she pardoned the usurper herself, it would be regarded as a sign of weakness which might have fatal results. When Mary said that she believed that Jane had been the innocent dupe of Northumberland and other unscrupulous men, Renard, knowing that Mary was well educated in the classics, reminded her of how Theodosius had executed not only Maximus, but also Maximus's young son Victor, when Maximus rebelled against him, because the interests of the State demanded it, although Victor was quite innocent.

But Mary would not accept his argument, and would only agree to the execution of three men for the plot to put Jane Grey on the throne. Northumberland and his two agents, Palmer and Gates, were put on trial for high treason in London, and were sentenced to death and beheaded on 22 August. Just before the execution, Northumberland converted to Catholicism, and wrote a recantation in which he renounced all the Protestant doctrines in which he had believed, and stated that it was these Protestant doctrines which had led him to commit high treason. Mary ordered that the widest publicity should be given to his recantation, and it caused consternation and considerable demoralisation among the Protestants. In later years, the Protestants were able to turn Northumberland's recantation to their own advantage, by arguing that it showed that the man who had governed England so corruptly under Edward VI and had committed high treason against Mary had always been a Catholic, and not a Protestant, at heart.

Mary was determined to overthrow the Protestant religion which had been established under Edward VI, and restore immediately the Mass and the religious settlement as it had

OPPOSITE A sixteenth-century chasuble, typical of the vestments the Protestants had confiscated in Edward VI's reign.

existed at the death of Henry VIII, though she was prepared to go a little more slowly about restoring the papal supremacy over the Church. Henry VIII's Act of Supremacy, which made the sovereign the Supreme Head of the Church of England, meant that this Supreme Head was now Mary herself; and however unwelcome the title and position might be to her, she was willing to use the power which it conferred on her to restore the Catholic religion before divesting herself of it and handing it over to the Pope. Renard, on Charles V's instructions, urged her not to do anything about changing religion until she had got rid of her political opponents and the country had settled down; but Mary refused to accept this advice. She told Renard that God had protected her during Edward's reign, when the heretics were in power; the government at that time knew very well that she attended Mass in secret, but they never arrested her or effectively interfered with her Mass, because God had answered her prayers and prevented the heretics from acting against her. She therefore owed it to God to show her gratitude by restoring the true religion in England immediately, though she added that she did not wish to force any man's conscience in matters of religion.

If Mary really meant what she said to Renard, and seriously intended to restore the Catholic religion while granting religious toleration to the Protestants, she was proposing to pursue a very unusual policy. It was accepted as a principle by all European rulers that it was for the sovereign to decide what religion he and his subjects were to adopt, and then to enforce the observance of this religion, and to forbid any other form of religious worship by the use of the criminal law. Eight years later, Catherine de'Medici tried the experiment of religious toleration in France. The result was not encouraging, because the Protestants, who had been cruelly persecuted for thirty years, used their newly-granted freedom to burn Catholic churches and murder Catholics, and in a very short time France was involved in a religious civil war which lasted until the end of the century.

Mary was determined to make England Catholic at once. The first difficulty arose about the funeral of Edward VI. Mary had always been fond of her brother, despite their religious differences, and she was eager to save his soul by giving him a Catholic funeral. Renard eventually persuaded her to give way

OPPOSITE Philip of Spain, the son of Charles V, was eleven years younger than Mary. Despite her reluctance to marry she became devoted to him.

The red velvet cover of Queen Mary's Psalter, embroidered with her emblem, the pomegranate. The psalter dates from the fourteenth century and was the property of Henry Manners, Lord Ross, who had been imprisoned by Mary for supporting Lady Jane Grey. In 1554 the psalter was being smuggled out of the country when it was discovered by a customs officer, who presented it to Mary.

on this point, by reminding her that as Edward had died a heretic he could not be given a Catholic funeral. On 8 August Edward was buried in Westminster Abbey with the Protestant funeral service of the Book of Common Prayer, although the funeral service, which rejected the Catholic doctrine of prayers for the dead, was one of the most radical and controversial sections of Cranmer's Prayer Book. Mary herself attended a Mass for Edward in private in the Tower.

132

But Mary would not allow the penal provisions of the Act of Uniformity to be enforced against the Catholics. Here she adopted a different attitude from that of the Protestants when they came to power. The Protestants, who had used Parliamentary statutes to introduce the religious Reformation under Henry VIII and Edward VI, had come to regard Acts of Parliament as binding law in all circumstances. When Edward VI, and later Elizabeth, came to the throne, they insisted on enforcing the old Catholic statutes of Henry VIII and Mary until they were repealed, and would not permit the Protestant extremists to defy the existing laws until these laws were changed. But Mary, when she first became Queen, would not permit the Protestant Acts of Parliament to be enforced against the Catholics, even though they had not yet been repealed. The later Protestant writers contrasted her attitude with that of Edward VI and Elizabeth to show how Protestants were more law-abiding than Catholics; but Mary, like Sir Thomas More and unlike the Protestants, did not recognise the validity of an Act of Parliament in all circumstances, and believed that a statute was void if it was found to conflict with the fundamental law of Christendom.

Sir James Hales, one of the judges of the Court of Common Pleas, came into conflict with Mary on this question. Sir James was a firm believer in the doctrine of the sovereignty of Parliament and the rule of law. He had braved the anger of Northumberland by refusing to subscribe to Edward VI's Will and the grant of the crown to Jane Grey, when all the other judges subscribed, because he argued that Edward's Will was illegal, as it conflicted with an Act of Parliament. Now, two months later, in August 1553, Hales went to Maidstone for the Assizes and proceeded to impose fines on Catholics who had broken the Act of Uniformity by attending Mass. Mary pardoned the convicted Catholics, and ordered Hales to stop enforcing the Act of Uniformity. Hales replied that as long as the Act of Parliament was unrepealed, it was his duty to enforce it, as the Queen's command could not alter the law. Mary then ordered him to be arrested, dismissed him from his office as judge, and imprisoned him in the King's Bench prison. He was released next year, and committed suicide.

The Protestant extremists, with that utter lack of political sense which characterises extremist fanatics, now played into Mary's hands and gave an opportunity to the most intolerant of the Catholics to take steps against the heretics. When these Protestants saw that Catholic priests were celebrating Mass in many churches in London, and that Mary was preventing the judges from prosecuting them, they preached at open-air pulpits and street corners in London, denouncing the Mass and calling on the government to enforce the Act of Uniformity against the Papists. Mary's first reaction was mild; she issued a proclamation on 12 August in which she deplored religious controversy between her subjects, and prohibited anyone from using the terms 'heretic' or 'Papist' in their sermons.

But next day, on Sunday 13 August, a prominent Catholic priest, Dr Bourn, preached at Mary's command at Paul's Cross. As always when official government preachers preached at the Cross, the Lord Mayor and the city officials sat in the front row around the open-air pulpit, and everyone waited for an official government pronouncement on some aspect of religion or politics. When Bourn began to uphold Catholic doctrines, he was heckled and shouted down by Protestants in the audience. The Lord Mayor indignantly appealed for order, but the tumult grew and developed into a riot, and someone threw a dagger at Bourn, which just missed him. Two well-known Protestant leaders, John Bradford and John Rogers, were in the audience. Rogers had helped Tyndale translate the first official English edition of the Bible which had been published under Henry VIII in 1537, though Henry afterwards, at Gardiner's suggestion, prevented the people from reading it. Bradford and Rogers calmed the crowd and escorted Bourn to safety.

The attack on Bourn was the excuse for which the hard-line elements in the government had been waiting. It aroused a great deal of indignation among the ordinary conservative Londoners. Bradford and Rogers were arrested and brought before the Privy Council and accused of inciting the riot. When they claimed that they had, on the contrary, calmed the rioters and saved Bourn's life, the Privy Councillors replied that though Bradford and Rogers had eventually done this, they had incited the riot in the earlier stages, and the fact that they had been able to calm the rioters, after the Lord Mayor had been unable to do so, showed that Bradford and Rogers were the recognised

Bradford

'Certen byshops talking
with maister Bradford in
pryson' from Foxe's
Book of Martyrs.

135

A goldsmith's workshop.
The Protestant refugees
whom Mary expelled
tended to be craftsmen or
small traders.

leaders of the rioters, and were responsible for the riot. They were committed to prison. During the last fortnight of August, some prominent Protestant leader was arrested in London nearly every day. At the beginning of September, the arrests spread to the provinces. Hooper was arrested in his diocese of Worcester, although six weeks earlier, with more religious consistency than political sense, he had exhorted the men of his diocese to fight for Mary against Jane Grey. Latimer, who had been a very prominent Protestant fifteen years before, but had retired from public life before the end of Edward's reign on account of his age and poor health, was arrested in the village in Warwickshire where he was living, and brought to London and imprisoned in the Tower.

On 14 September, later than many people had expected, it was Cranmer's turn. He had been left in freedom in Lambeth Palace for two months after Mary's victory; but at the beginning of September he allowed himself to be persuaded by the Protestant Bishop of Rochester, Scory, to issue a public declaration criticising the Mass. This in itself was not an offence; but, as a result, Cranmer was summoned before the Privy Council and charged with high treason in supporting Jane Grey's usurpation of the crown. Some of the members of the Council who were present on this occasion had been more active than Cranmer in supporting Jane Grey; but they sent him to the Tower on this charge of high treason.

Mary was encouraged to proceed in her measures to restore the Catholic religion by the support which she received from the clergy. At the meeting of Convocation in October, a resolution calling for the restoration of the Catholic Mass was carried with only six dissentient votes, after the presiding Prolocutor, Hugh Weston, had made a speech in praise of Mary, whom he referred to as 'Mary the Virgin'. Two prominent Protestant theologians, John Taylor and Philpot, were not allowed to speak against the Mass, and were forcibly thrown out of the building. Many former Protestants were converting to Catholicism. The success of the popular rising in Mary's favour had convinced many people that God was on her side. The slogan '*Vox populi, vox Dei*' appeared on walls and at crossroads all over the country.

Mary now made two very popular moves. She announced

that she would not collect the taxes which had been voted, at Northumberland's insistence, in the last Parliament of Edward VI; and she expelled all the foreign Protestant refugees from England. In the reign of Edward VI, French, Dutch and Flemish Protestants, and a sprinkling of Protestants from countries further afield, had come to England to escape from the religious persecution which they were suffering in their own countries. A few of the refugees were learned theologians who stayed with Cranmer at Lambeth Palace; but most of them were artisans or small tradesmen. A colony of weavers had been established at Glastonbury in Somerset; but most of the refugees stayed in London, where they became very unpopular with the ordinary Londoner. The English Catholics complained that, under Edward VI, England had become 'a harbour for all infidelity'; but the chief objection of the man in the street was simply that they were foreigners, because, in the sixteenth century, the English people were well-known to be very hostile to all foreigners.

Mary's decision to expel the refugees was therefore very popular with most of her subjects. Like other refugees in later centuries, the foreign Protestants who were expelled from England afterwards thought that they had been lucky to get out before the government started killing them; but at the time it caused great hardship. In most cases they were not allowed to take their property with them, and ran the risk of being arrested and burned as heretics when they returned from their English refuge to their country of origin. Most of them were the Emperor's subjects, and faced the savage persecution in the Netherlands when they reached Antwerp. Mary arranged with Renard for her officers to inform the Emperor's officers in the Netherlands of the ships in which the refugees would be travelling, so that the authorities in the Netherlands could meet them and arrest them as soon as they landed.

Mary had also to deal with the problem of the Protestant clergy in the parishes all over south-eastern England. This was more serious than it would otherwise have been because of the different attitudes of the Protestants and the Catholics towards the marriage of priests. In the four years since the marriage of priests had been legalised in England, many parish priests had married; and although most of them might otherwise have been prepared to convert back to Catholicism when Mary became Queen, they could not alter the fact that they had married. The marriage of priests outraged the Catholic clergy almost more than anything else, and large sections of the general public were equally shocked at it. Before the Reformation, many priests had been living more or less openly with concubines; but there was a difference, in the eyes of the authorities and the people, between merely committing a sin, and openly asserting that the sin was not a sin at all. So Mary and her bishops considered that the marriage of priests was much worse than the old concubinage, and the parish priests, who in many cases had married the concubines with whom they had lived for many years, were now punished for it. Mary was particularly indignant at the conduct of those married priests who had been monks before the dissolution of the monasteries. She considered that monks and nuns who had married were guilty of a much greater offence than the priests who had done so, because monks and nuns had taken vows of celibacy, whereas priests, though compelled to remain celibate by the laws of the Church, had not for many centuries taken any oath of celibacy at their ordination.

Mary ordered that all married priests were to be deprived of their benefices. Those who had been monks were ordered to separate from their wives and children, and not to make any attempt to see them again. Those who had not been monks were given the choice, either to put away their wives, in which case they would be given a new benefice in a different parish after doing penance, or to keep their wives and be debarred from ever holding any ecclesiastical position; and Mary did not allow the deprived clergy any pension like the pensions which Henry VIII had paid to the monks of the suppressed monasteries. The number of married priests who were affected by this order was about twenty per cent, on average, in the dioceses of south-eastern England, but in London, Essex and Norfolk it was higher, about one-third of the parish priests being deprived. Nearly twenty per cent of the clergy were deprived in the diocese of Bath and Wells, because in the last twenty years Protestantism had spread beyond the confines of south-eastern England. There were Protestants in the dioceses of Worcester and Lichfield, and also in Devon and the south-west, and in

South Wales. But Protestantism had made no progress north of the Trent.

Many of the married clergy agreed to put away their wives, and all over England, in the spring of 1554, processions were held, through the streets of the towns, with the penitent priest being flogged, as he walked, by his bishop or by the clergy who accompanied him. Popular hatred of the married clergy was aroused by sermons, and by a pamphlet written by a layman, Miles Huggarde, a small tradesman living in London, who explained away the whole Reformation by the theory that the immoral Protestants wished to have an excuse to marry and satisfy their lust for women; and he denounced all priests' wives as promiscuous harlots. Severe punishment was inflicted on priests who, having put away their wives, renewed a connexion with them. In the spring of 1554 the constables in London, when investigating a robbery, found the vicar of a church in Cheapside in a house together with his former wife, and both he and she were imprisoned in separate prisons; and at Easter 1556 a priest in the diocese of Lincoln, who had been married and had put away his wife, was imprisoned because he had been seen carrying his small son in his arms.

On 1 October 1553 Mary was crowned by Gardiner in Westminster Abbey after the traditional procession through the streets from the Tower. No sooner was the coronation over than Renard, who had given Mary a few weeks' respite before the ceremony, renewed his pressure on her to marry Philip of Spain, and to execute the traitors who had supported Jane Grey. In November she gave way to his demands to the extent of ordering that Jane Grey, her husband Guilford Dudley, Lord Henry and Lord Ambrose Dudley, and Cranmer, should be put on trial for high treason for their support of Jane's usurpation of the crown. But Mary was determined that they should have a fair trial. She told Chief Justice Morgan that she disapproved of the practice by which witnesses for the defence were intimidated and discouraged from giving evidence against the Crown at treason trials, and ordered Morgan to allow such evidence to be given.

Jane Grey, the Dudleys and Cranmer pleaded guilty, and were sentenced to death. But Mary would not sign the warrants for their execution, though she did not pardon them, but kept them in the Tower, uncertain of their fate. There were no more trials, and some of Jane's most prominent supporters, like her father Suffolk, had been pardoned and released from prison. But Mary was a little capricious in her choice as to who was to be pardoned and who was to be reserved for punishment. She seems almost to have acted on the principle that those individuals who had done her injury in the past were to be forgiven, while those who had rendered her some service were to be victimised. Cranmer, who had been more reluctant than any of the other Privy Councillors to subscribe to Edward VI's Will granting the crown to Jane Grey, and who had interceded with Henry VIII for Mary's life, was sentenced to death for treason; and Justice Hales, the only judge who had refused to subscribe to Edward's Will, was the only judge whom Mary arrested. But Norfolk, who had treated her so badly in 1536, and Rich, whose perjured evidence had convicted Sir Thomas More, and who had arrested Mary's servants for celebrating Mass at the time of his visit to Copthall in 1551, were both appointed by Mary to be members of her Privy Council. Perhaps she convinced herself, by this policy, that she disregarded all personal feelings of gratitude and revenge, and rewarded and punished only in the interests of her realm and subjects.

Mary was more ready now than she had been a few months earlier to listen to Renard's suggestion that she should arrest Elizabeth and get Parliament to pass an Act altering the succession to the crown, as established in the Act of 1544 and Henry VIII's Will, so as to exclude Elizabeth. In August 1553 Mary had a talk with Elizabeth, and urged her to go to Mass. Elizabeth refused. Mary renewed the pressure, and on the Feast of the Nativity of the Virgin, on 8 September, Elizabeth went to Mass; but she did not go again. Some people believed that Elizabeth's half-hearted compliance was nicely calculated, so that although she would save her life by going to Mass, she would show her Protestant supporters, by her reluctance, that she was a Protestant at heart. If this was really what Elizabeth was trying to do, she was playing a dangerous game. Her attitude aroused Mary's deepest suspicions. Mary was convinced that Elizabeth, even though she might pretend to become a Catholic, was really a Protestant, and that if she became Queen she would make England a Protestant state again. But despite her misgivings, Mary would not arrest Elizabeth, or introduce legislation to exclude her from the crown.

When Parliament met in October 1553, two important statutes were passed. One annulled the divorce of Henry VIII and Catherine of Aragon, and enacted that Mary was Henry's legitimate daughter; the other restored the Mass throughout England as from 21 December, and suppressed the Book of Common Prayer and made it illegal to attend a Protestant service. In December, some Protestants succeeded in getting into Mary's presence-chamber at Whitehall and depositing there the corpse of a dog, with its head shaved like a priest's, its ears clipped and a rope around its neck. Mary sent a message to Parliament in which she warned her subjects that such acts would compel her to adopt harsh repressive measures. But the heresy statutes, under which heretics could be burned, were not re-enacted in this Parliament.

Renard was not finding it easy to persuade Mary to agree to the Emperor's suggestion that she should marry Philip of Spain. She told Renard that she thought that she was too old for Philip, as she was thirty-seven, and Philip was a young man of twenty-six. Renard said that a man of twenty-six could hardly be called a young man, but was rather middle-aged, because at forty a man was old, and few men survived beyond the age of fifty or sixty. Mary then explained what was really on her mind: a man of twenty-six was likely to feel amorous, and this she would not like. She promised Renard that if she did marry Philip, she would fall very deeply in love with him, because the Church commanded a wife to love her husband, but she would not do so out of any carnal desire. Mary knew that, however much the idea of sex disgusted her, it was her duty to submit to it in order to have a child who would exclude Elizabeth from the throne; and this conflict between her duty and her instincts caused her great distress. On 28 October 1553 she received Renard in the presence of four of her Privy Councillors – Gardiner, Arundel, Paget and Petre, the Secretary of State. She told them that she had wept for more than two hours that morning, praying to God to inspire her in her decision about her marriage. Next day, which was a Sunday, Renard again visited Mary, with no one else being present except Mary's

OPPOSITE Princess Elizabeth in a portrait by an unknown artist.

142

lady-in-waiting, Mrs Clarentius. Mary told Renard that since he had first raised the question of the marriage at Newhall, when she was on her way to London from Framlingham, she had not slept, because she lay awake worrying about it. Then she suddenly went to the corner of the room, where the Holy Sacrament was hanging, and, kneeling before it, prayed aloud for guidance. Mrs Clarentius knelt and prayed beside her, and Renard, after a moment's hesitation, did so too.

After Mary had overcome her physical repugnance to the idea of marriage, there were still the political difficulties. The French ambassador in London, Noailles, wrote to his King that Mary followed the advice of the Emperor's ambassador in everything, and often met him in secret, without the knowledge of her Privy Council, to arrange about her marriage to Philip; but she did not, by any means, comply with all Renard's demands about the marriage, and referred him to Gardiner to bargain about the terms of the marriage contract. Gardiner had acquired considerable experience of foreign affairs during the many years when he was a minister of Henry VIII's, and had been sent on many diplomatic missions abroad by Henry. He had always favoured an alliance with the Netherlands and the Empire, rather than with France, and was now strongly in favour of an alliance with Charles V. But he realised the danger of England falling under Spanish domination if Mary married a Spanish prince, and knew that English xenophobia would be aroused at any suggestion that such a thing might occur. He therefore insisted on inserting all kinds of complicated guarantees into the marriage treaty. At first he made the unprecedented suggestion that Philip, after he married Mary, should be named after Mary in all state documents, which should be issued in the name of 'Mary and Philip, Queen and King of England', etc. Renard rejected this proposal as derogatory to Philip's honour, and Gardiner and the English Councillors agreed that he should be named first; but Renard gave way on nearly every other point. He agreed that none of Philip's Spanish advisers should interfere in English affairs, and that Philip and Mary should be advised on all matters relating to England by English-born ministers only. He also agreed that England should not be required to declare war on France, with whom the Emperor was at war, or to break off diplomatic relations with France.

Although Mary, as the bride, would normally have been expected to provide the dowry, Charles sent gifts of silver from the Mexican mines to England, and Mary had much the best of the bargain as regards the financial arrangements.

When all the other difficulties had been overcome, Mary raised another objection. She refused to be married in Lent. The laws of the Church prohibited marriages in Lent, but Renard was sure that there would be no difficulty in obtaining a dispensation from the Pope in the case of Philip and Mary. But Mary refused to apply for a dispensation to be married in Lent, though she was prepared to ask for the necessary papal dispensation to enable her to marry Philip although he was her cousin.

On 2 January 1554 Count Egmont, who later became a hero of the national and Protestant resistance in the Netherlands to Philip of Spain, arrived in London with his colleague Count Lalaing to complete the negotiations for the marriage of Philip and Mary. But the English hatred of foreigners, which had worked in Mary's favour when she expelled the Protestant refugees, worked against her in connexion with the Spanish marriage. As soon as rumours about it got around, it caused great resentment among the people. When Egmont and Lalaing arrived in London, they were pelted with snowballs as they rode through the streets, and there were hostile demonstrations in front of their lodgings. Mary was incensed, and gave orders that anyone who insulted the Emperor's representatives was to be severely punished. But the government did not realise the strength of the opposition to the marriage, and were taken unprepared when a revolt broke out in Kent at the end of January 1554.

The revolt was led by Sir Thomas Wyatt, a gentleman living at Allington in Kent, whose father had been a leading diplomat and poet at the Court of Henry VIII. Wyatt was joined by several Kentish gentlemen and by many of the common people, and was soon at the head of five thousand men. Kent was a county in which Protestant feeling was strong, and most of Wyatt's followers were Protestants; but he did not put forward any religious demands, and asked only that Mary's marriage to Philip should not take place. One or two ardent Protestants joined Mary's forces and fought against Wyatt; but she had much less support from the Protestants than she had had at the time of her struggle with Jane Grey, and there was a good deal of truth in the Catholic allegation that the Wyatt rebellion was a Protestant insurrection, although many Protestants still refused to fight against their lawful sovereign, even if she was a Papist.

Mary assembled a force of men-at-arms and the London trainbands and sent them against Wyatt at Rochester under the command of the old Duke of Norfolk; but many of Norfolk's men deserted to Wyatt, and within a week the rebels were in Southwark. Mary advised Egmont and Lalaing that their lives were in danger, and they hurriedly left England; but, on Gardiner's advice, she refused to ask the Emperor for military aid, or to engage any foreign mercenaries. She relied on the loyalty of the people of London. She left St James's Palace, where she had been staying, and took refuge in London, within the protection of London Wall and its fortifications; and on 1 February she addressed the Lord Mayor and Aldermen at the Guildhall, and called on her loyal subjects to fight for their Queen against the traitor Wyatt. The men of the sixteenth century did not expect to see acts of leadership and determination from women; and Mary impressed those who heard her, by her courage and coolness at the Guildhall, as deeply as her sister Elizabeth did at Tilbury thirty-four years later when she faced the danger of invasion from Philip of Spain's Armada. Her words at the Guildhall were recorded by her great enemy, John Foxe.

> I am your Queen [she said], to whom at my coronation, when I was wedded to the realm and laws of the same (the spousal ring whereof I have on my finger, which never hitherto was, nor hereafter shall be, left off), you promised your allegiance and obedience unto me. ... And I say to you, on the word of a Prince, I cannot tell how naturally the mother loveth the child, for I was never the mother of any; but certainly, if a Prince and Governor may as naturally and earnestly love her subjects as the mother doth love the child, then assure yourselves that I, being your lady and mistress, do as earnestly and tenderly love and favour you. And I, thus loving you, cannot but think that ye as heartily and faithfully love me; and then I doubt not but we shall give these rebels a short and speedy overthrow.

Mary's words, which were as politically skilful as they were

An Italian pamphlet telling the story of Wyatt's rebellion.

146

COPIA

D'VNA LETTERA VENVTA DI LONDRA DALLA CORTE DELLA REGINA D'INGHILTERRA.

Doue narra, il fatto d'arme fatto fra la Regina, e i ſuoi ribelli, con il nome di tutti li Capi principali di detti
ribelli, & la cauſa donde e proceduta la ribellio
ne, con la mortalita de l'uno & l'altro eſ
ſercito, con il numero delli prigioni
fatti dalla Regina, e la giuſtitia
ch'eſſa a fatto, e fa di gior
no in giorno, contra
di detti ribelli.
Et vna Oratione belliſſima, fatta da detta Regina, in pu-
blico a tutto il Popolo di Londra, & a tutti
Capi del Regno d'Inghilterra.

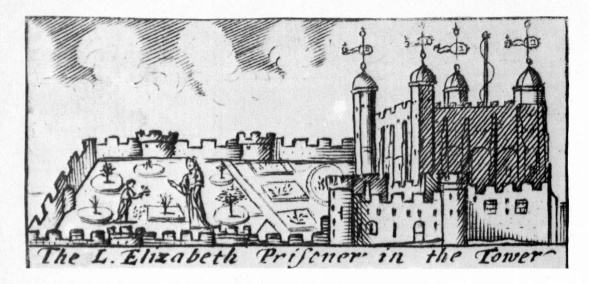

The L. Elizabeth Prisoner in the Tower

morally courageous, inspired the citizens of London, and twenty-five thousand men enrolled to defend their Queen against Wyatt. When Wyatt and his seven thousand men found that London Bridge was manned by Londoners who were loyal to Mary, they marched to Kingston, where they crossed the river, and advanced on London from the west, reaching Hyde Park Corner, about two miles from the walls of the city. Mary's commanders allowed Wyatt to advance as far as Ludgate Hill, and then hemmed him in and overwhelmed him; and he surrendered, and the rebellion collapsed. Meanwhile, the Duke of Suffolk had tried to start another revolt in the Midlands in support of Wyatt; but this failed much more ignominiously than Wyatt's rising. Suffolk fled to his estates in Warwickshire, but was betrayed by his gamekeeper, and was discovered hiding in a tree, and sent to the Tower.

The Wyatt rebellion had very serious repercussions for the Protestants and all Mary's political opponents. It brought about a complete change in Mary's attitude, and convinced her that Renard had been right when he had warned her that her leniency to Jane Grey's followers would be interpreted as an act of weakness and would encourage fresh sedition. Renard gave her a French translation of Thucydides, and drew her attention to the advice which Thucydides gives as to how to deal with rebels; but this was unnecessary. Mary assured Renard that 'she would not cease to demand of the law to strike

148

The L. Elizabeth before her Sister Q. Mary

terror into all those who ventured to do evil'. She was now
ready to listen to the Machiavellian theory of Renard and
Gardiner that a prince owed a duty to his subjects to act with
severity, not only against those guilty of treason, but also
against those who were potentially dangerous to the state, in
order to save his subjects from the curse of civil war.

Within a week of the collapse of Wyatt's rebellion, Mary
signed a warrant for the execution of Jane Grey and Guilford
Dudley on the charge of high treason on which they had been
convicted in November, and they were beheaded on 12
February. Jane, who was only sixteen, was certainly not
involved in any way in Wyatt's insurrection, and was as guilty,
and no more so, than she had been six months earlier when
Mary was firmly resolved that she would not put her to death;
but Mary had now been persuaded to act on the principles of
expediency, not justice. Cranmer was not executed under the
sentence of treason of November, because Mary had decided to
proceed against him for heresy instead. On 18 March, Elizabeth
was arrested and sent to the Tower on a charge of complicity in
Wyatt's rebellion. Mary had thus taken the step against Elizabeth
which neither her father nor her brother had quite ventured to
take against Mary herself; she had arrested the heir to the throne
on a charge of high treason.

Elizabeth was imprisoned in the Tower for two months.
Wyatt was repeatedly questioned in an effort to get him to

149

incriminate Elizabeth and say that she was a party to the plot; but he insisted that she had had no part in it, and when he was executed on 11 April, he stated, in his speech from the scaffold, that Elizabeth was innocent. He was almost certainly speaking the truth. The French Ambassador, Noailles, had followed recent events with great interest, having pinned his hopes on Wyatt's success as the only way of preventing England from falling under the Emperor's control; but though Noailles was exceptionally well-informed, and had some discreet contacts with Wyatt's supporters, he did not believe that Elizabeth had anything to do with the rebels. It had, however, been Wyatt's intention to make Elizabeth Queen instead of Mary, and to marry her to Edward Courtenay, whom Mary had released from the Tower when she arrived in London from Framlingham. After seven months of freedom – the only freedom he had enjoyed since the age of twelve – he was re-arrested at Mary's orders, and taken back to the Tower.

About 120 people were executed for their part in the Wyatt rebellion. The Duke of Suffolk, who had never been put on trial for his support of his daughter's usurpation of the crown, was now tried for high treason for his attempted revolt in the Midlands, and was beheaded. A random selection of the rank-and-file were executed, and their corpses could be seen hanging from gibbets in many parts of London. Some of them, after being sentenced to death, petitioned Mary for mercy; but she ordered the death sentence to be carried out in every case. Another four hundred, whom the authorities had decided to pardon, were brought to the courtyard of the palace at Whitehall with halters round their necks, and begged on their knees for mercy; and Mary appeared at the palace window, and pardoned them. In April Sir Nicholas Throckmorton was tried for high treason at the Guildhall on a charge of complicity in Wyatt's revolt. Throckmorton claimed to be the man who had warned Mary to escape from Hunsdon in July 1553 when Northumberland was about to arrest her; but he was a convinced Protestant. He defended himself so ably at his trial that the jury brought in a verdict of not guilty. Mary ordered him to be detained in prison, and arrested all the members of the jury and imprisoned them by her royal command, for having returned a perverse verdict. The power to imprison subjects by order of the Queen and Council was exercised by all the Tudor sovereigns, and was not challenged by anyone until the seventeenth century; but the practice of imprisoning jurors for returning a wrong verdict, though not as outrageous as it would be today, was unusual, and caused adverse comment at the time. Mary released Throckmorton a year later, and allowed him to emigrate to France. In Elizabeth's reign, he became one of the most skilful and important of the English diplomats.

Mary did not, in the end, put Elizabeth on trial for treason. After all the investigations had been concluded, no evidence had been found which implicated Elizabeth in the revolt. Elizabeth was aged twenty – the same age that Mary was when she renounced the papal supremacy and admitted the invalidity of her mother's marriage; and Elizabeth dissembled as well as Mary had done in 1536. Renard and Gardiner were nevertheless convinced that it was essential that Elizabeth should be executed. They tried to influence Mary by reminding her that Elizabeth was a secret heretic, that if Mary died childless Elizabeth would become Queen and overthrow the Catholic religion, and that this was an opportunity, which would probably never recur, of preventing her from succeeding to the crown by cutting off her head.

In her new pitiless mood, Mary might have agreed to do this; but there were other reasons, apart from the Queen's hesitation, which prevented Elizabeth's execution. Elizabeth was very popular in the country; and there was a strong party in Mary's Privy Council which was opposed to proceeding against her. It was led by Paget and Pembroke, who had played such a decisive part in the defeat of Jane Grey. Paget and his supporters warned Mary that if Elizabeth were put on trial for high treason, with no evidence against her, it was very doubtful whether a jury would convict her, and it was equally doubtful whether Parliament could be persuaded to pass an Act of Attainder under which she could be executed. It would no doubt have been possible to get her convicted by some special commission, but this would have been a very unpopular move. Renard reluctantly accepted the position, and decided that, in view of Elizabeth's popularity in the country, it would be more dangerous to put her to death than to leave her alive. After keeping Elizabeth in the Tower for two months, Mary allowed her to go to her house at Woodstock in Oxfordshire, and be held there under stringent house arrest. Mary also released Courtenay from the Tower, and allowed him to go to Italy, where he died.

The Wyatt rebellion, as well as persuading Mary to follow Renard's advice about punishing traitors, persuaded Renard to abandon his opposition to Mary's plans to proceed against the heretics. If Mary had seriously considered, in 1553, granting religious toleration to the Protestants, this was another of the merciful intentions which she abandoned after the Wyatt rebellion. Gardiner and his party wished to persecute the Protestant heretics who denied transubstantiation as relentlessly as they had persecuted them in the reign of Henry VIII, and he and Renard felt that, after the defeat of Wyatt, they were strong enough to proceed against the most eminent of the Protestants. In April 1554 Cranmer, Ridley and Latimer were taken from the Tower to Oxford, and required to take part in a theological disputation about transubstantiation with Catholic theologians. In form, the disputation was a theological debate, conducted under the formal rules of disputations, but the presiding Prolocutor, Weston, who was a violent Catholic partisan, had been granted a commission by Mary under which he was to decide whether or not the doctrines put forward by Cranmer, Ridley and Latimer were heretical. Oxford, unlike Cambridge, had always been a Catholic centre, and now, in their hour of triumph, a thousand Catholic supporters filled the spectators' seats at the disputation in the Divinity School, and jeered and interrupted the three Protestants, as they defended their position with great intellectual skill. After the disputation had lasted three days, Weston condemned them as heretics.

Many people expected that Mary would now give orders for Cranmer, Ridley and Latimer to be burned; but when the question was discussed in the Privy Council on 2 May, objections were raised. The heresy Act of 1401, and Henry VIII's statutes against heretics, had been repealed by Edward VI's government in 1547, and there was no longer any statute in force which authorised the Queen to burn heretics. Despite this, two Protestant extremists had been burned by Northumberland's government in 1550 and 1551 for denying the doctrine of the Trinity, as Northumberland had been advised by Rich, his Lord

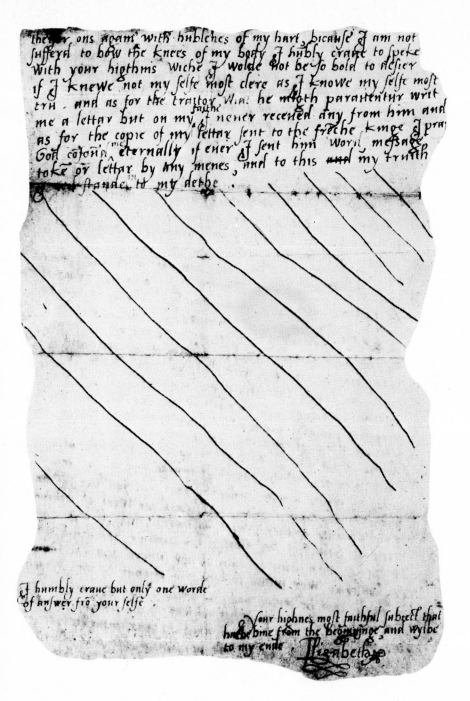

thervr ons again with hublches of my hart, because I am not
suffered to bow the knees of my body I hubly crave to speke
with your higthnis wiche I wolde not be so bold to desier
if I knewe not my selfe most clere as I knowe my selfe most
trw. and as for the traitor Wiat he migth paraventur writ
me a lettar but on my faithe I never receued any from him and
as for the copie of my lettar sent to the freche kinge I pray
God cofoun me eternally if euer I sent him worde message
toke or lettar by any menes, and to this my truith
I stande it my dethe.

I humbly craue but only one worde
of answer fro your selfe.

Your highnes most faithful subiect that
hathe bine from the beginninge and wyl be
to my ende. Elizabeth

The last paragraph of a letter from Elizabeth to Mary protesting her innocence of involvement with the Wyatt rebellion. Elizabeth wrote this while she was waiting to be taken to the Tower by barge. Lines were drawn across the blank space to prevent forgers adding a recantation or confession.

153

THOMAS. CRANMER, BIS
. MARTIR .

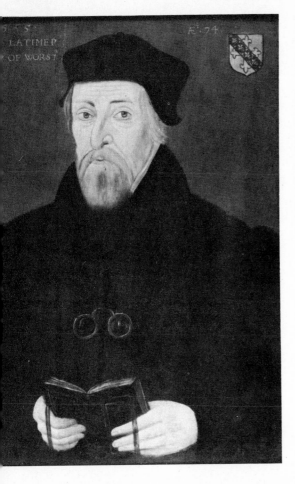

Chancellor, that it was legal for the King to burn heretics under the Common Law, independently of any Act of Parliament. But now several members of Mary's Privy Council, and the judges, expressed doubt as to whether this was legal; so Mary decided not to burn Cranmer, Ridley and Latimer until Parliament had re-enacted the heresy statutes.

In April 1554 the government introduced a bill in Parliament to re-enact the heresy Act of 1401, under which the Queen would have power to order the burning of any person who had been condemned as a heretic by an ecclesiastical court or royal commission. Mary was shocked to find that there was considerable opposition in both Houses, though Gardiner used all his influence to get the bill through. The opposition seems to have been secretly organised by Paget. It is not clear whether he was

Thomas Cranmer (far left), Hugh Latimer (left) and Nicholas Ridley (above), the three eminent bishops whose deaths were to be an inspiration to Protestantism in England.

155

trying to hold up the burning of heretics for as long as possible because he favoured a moderate policy, or whether he was only interested in his personal struggle for power with Gardiner, who was the leader of the hard-liners in the Privy Council; but Paget first opposed the bill in the House of Lords, and then supported it after he had had a long private talk with Mary.

There was another factor involved. The peers and the country gentlemen and the representatives of the boroughs who sat in Parliament had converted to Catholicism and were going to Mass; but they were worried about the rumours which they had heard that the Queen was intending to restore the property of the monasteries, especially if there was any truth in the other rumour, that she was planning to restore the Pope's authority over the Church of England. They therefore decided to try to make an unofficial bargain with Mary, by which they would re-enact the heresy laws and allow her to burn Protestants on condition that she did not deprive them of the former monastic lands which they had bought from Henry VIII. In May 1554 the bill to restore the Act for the Burning of Heretics passed the House of Commons, but was defeated in the House of Lords.

Meanwhile Mary had been taking the final steps for her marriage to Philip of Spain. After the Wyatt rebellion had been suppressed, Egmont and Lalaing returned to England to solemnise the engagement of Philip to Mary. The ceremony took place in a room at Whitehall, with Egmont acting as Philip's proxy. Before the proceedings began, Mary went to the corner of the room, where the Sacrament was hanging, and throwing herself on her knees before the Host, called loudly on God to witness that she was not marrying out of lust or carnal desire, but only out of her sense of duty to her kingdom and her subjects.

In July 1554 Prince Philip of Spain sailed for England from Corunna to marry Mary. He landed at Southampton in heavy rain on Friday 20 July. He was welcomed with great ceremony by Gardiner and most of the English nobility, and on 23 July he rode to Winchester, where Mary was waiting for him. He lodged in the Mayor's house, and Mary in Gardiner's palace. That evening, Philip visited Mary in secret, and they met for the first time; and next morning, he went in state, with his escort, to be officially introduced to her. They were married on 25 July,

St James's Day, by Gardiner in his episcopal church. Philip, dressed in white, arrived at the door of the cathedral, where Mary kept him waiting for more than half an hour. When she arrived, dressed in cloth-of-gold, with the sword of state borne before her, she was officially betrothed to Philip at a ceremony at the cathedral door, after which the Count of Figueroa, as Charles v's representative, read out a letter from Charles in which he declared that he was giving Philip the kingdom of Naples as a wedding present. As Philip was now not merely Prince of Spain, but King of Naples, he, too, had to have a sword of state carried before him, like Mary, and everyone had to wait until a second sword of state was brought for Philip. Then Philip and Mary walked up the aisle, and were married by Gardiner in a ceremony which lasted from twelve noon to 3 p.m. They left the cathedral and walked hand in hand to the palace, where they had a banquet, at which only Philip and Mary sat and ate, while all the lords of the realm waited upon them. The banquet lasted till 6 p.m., and was followed by a programme of music; but the King and Queen and all the nobles had retired to bed before 9 p.m.

Philip and Mary then travelled in state to London. Philip's handsome presence, his gallant manners, and his generosity in the distribution of largesse almost succeeded in winning the hearts of the people who saw him; and either because of this, or because of fear, there were no hostile demonstrations against him. But his Spanish gentlemen who came with him immediately began to feel the hostility of the English people to foreigners, though they had received orders to make themselves agreeable to everyone, and tried their best, under considerable provocation, to carry out these instructions. The English jostled the Spaniards in the street, and refused to let lodgings to them. The Spaniards were very disappointed with the ladies at Mary's Court. They complained that none of them was beautiful, and that most of them were downright ugly; and though they saw many pretty English women in the streets, they were shocked at the immodest way in which the women hooked up their skirts and showed their stockings as they walked.

Mary had always intended to restore the papal supremacy over the Church of England. As soon as she became Queen she opened secret negotiations with the Pope about this. The Pope

ABOVE The chair used by Mary during her marriage to Philip in Winchester Cathedral (left).

'The kissing coin' commemorating the wedding of Mary and Philip.

appointed Cardinal Pole to be his legate in England. Reginald Pole was a distant relative of Mary's. His mother, the Countess of Salisbury, was the daughter of the Duke of Clarence, the brother of Edward IV, and had been Mary's godmother at her confirmation when she was born. She had afterwards been executed as a Papist traitor by Henry VIII. Pole, in his youth, had been in favour with Henry, but he disapproved of the divorce of Catherine of Aragon and the break with Rome, and he went abroad. From his exile, he wrote a number of letters to Henry in which he criticised Henry's religious policy. This criticism, coming from a man of Pole's rank and intellectual eminence, had enraged Henry, who had spent a surprising amount of effort and money in employing agents to assassinate Pole in Italy. Pole had become an influential figure in Rome and had been created a Cardinal, though he had been criticised in certain quarters there for being too soft with heretics.

In the autumn of 1553 Pole was living in a monastery on the shores of Lake Garda, and from here he conducted a lengthy correspondence with Mary which went on for over a year. He called on her, as a true daughter of the Church, to undo the evil which her father had committed and reintroduce papal supremacy in England. Charles v and Renard tried to persuade Mary that Pole was a well-meaning but impractical enthusiast who did not appreciate the political difficulties of taking such a step. Mary wrote sadly to Pole that though she was most eager to do as he advised, he must realise that she could not move as fast as she would wish because of the political difficulties; and she was much distressed when he replied that no political difficulties should be allowed to stand in the way of the service of God, and asked her whether 'that other Mary' would have refused to admit St Peter to her house. Mary wrote to Pole that it would be easier for her to persuade her Parliament and people to accept papal supremacy if Pole would get the Pope to confirm the grant of the monastic lands to the present owners; but Pole found this suggestion shocking. Pole set out for England to plead St Peter's cause with Mary; but Charles v succeeded, by one pretext after another, in detaining him in his territories. Eventually, after Mary had shown considerable tact and patience for a year in dealing with Pole on the one hand and the Emperor's ambassador on the other, she persuaded Renard, Philip and Charles v that there would be no danger in re-uniting the realm with Rome, and persuaded Pole and the Pope to confirm the ownership of the monastic lands by the gentlemen. She herself returned to the religious orders the houses and lands of the monasteries which Henry viii had seized and had retained for himself, and monasteries and convents were re-established at Westminster, Greenwich, Sheen, Sion and elsewhere; but no other monastery was restored.

In November 1554 Pole travelled in state, as Papal Legate, from Brussels to Dover, where he was received with great pomp by several members of the Privy Council. A few days before he arrived, someone remembered that the Act of Attainder which had been passed in 1538, under which Pole was condemned as a traitor and sentenced to death, was still in force, and Parliament hastily repealed the Act while the former traitor was being triumphantly escorted from Dover to London. On 24 November he came in his barge in the gloomy weather up the river from Gravesend to Westminster, and was received by

The two sides of a medal
celebrating the
restoration of the power of
the Papacy in England.
The Pope depicted is
Julius III.

Philip and Mary in Whitehall. He saluted Mary with the words
of the *Ave Maria* – 'Hail Mary full of grace!' – and then went to
the House of Lords, where he addressed the peers and members
of the House of Commons. On 29 November Parliament
passed the bill repealing Henry VIII's Act of Supremacy and
restoring the supremacy of the Pope over the Church of
England; the bill passed unanimously in the House of Lords,
and with only two dissentient votes in the House of Commons.
Next day Pole absolved the realm from the sin of schism, and
proclaimed, in the Pope's name, that 30 November should be

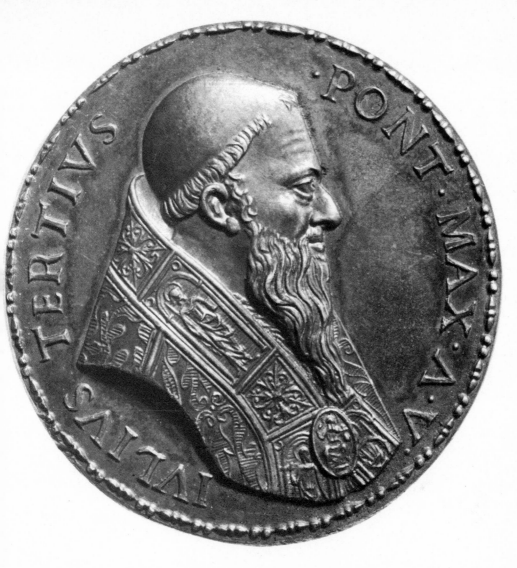

celebrated as a new holy day in the Church calendar, the Feast
of the Reconciliation. By Christmas Parliament had passed 'An
Act for the Renewing of Three Statutes made for the Punishment of Heresies', which re-enacted the Act for the Burning of
Heretics of 1401. The bill passed through all its stages in both
Houses, unanimously, in six days. At last the burning of heretics
could begin.

O Lord strengthen them

...William...

7
The Burning
of the
Heretics
1554-8

WITH THE REALM RE-UNITED WITH ROME, and the heresy Act on the statute book, Mary needed one more thing – an heir who would exclude Elizabeth from the throne, and who would be brought up as a Catholic and would preserve the Catholic religion in England after Mary's death. In September 1554, two months after her marriage, she informed her Council that she was pregnant. At Christmas she said that she had felt the child move in her womb for the first time when Pole came to Whitehall on 24 November, at the moment when she first saw the Legate's cross; she stated that on that occasion, 'the pious child exulted in the womb'.

She was examined by the Court physicians, all of whom expressed the opinion that the Queen was indeed pregnant; and everyone could see that her womb had swollen. But there were rumours at Court that the report was not true. The French ambassador heard, from a reliable source close to the Queen's bedchamber, that the chief midwife had told a friend, in strict confidence, that Mary could not possibly be pregnant, because, apart from the swelling of the womb, she had none of the physical symptoms of pregnancy. The midwife thought that the doctors must either be very ignorant, or else that they knew very well that Mary was not pregnant, but were afraid to say so.

Renard was anxious.

> Sire, everything in this kingdom depends on the Queen's safe deliverance [he wrote to Charles V]. If God is pleased to grant her a child, things will take a turn for the better. If not, I foresee trouble on so great a scale that the pen can hardly set it down. Certain it is that the order of succession has been so badly decided that the Lady Elizabeth comes next, and that means heresy again, and the true religion overthrown.

On 30 April the rumour spread in London that Mary had given birth to a son. Without any orders having been received from any authority, the bells were rung in jubilation in most of the London churches, and bonfires were lit in the streets. The news from London reached Spain, where Charles V's daughter Joanna, the Regent of Spain, sent her congratulations on the birth of the Prince to her brother King Philip. But the child did not come. It was then announced that a mistake had been made, and that the baby would be born in June. The people waited for the official announcement of the birth, but no

A prayer for pregnant women, said to be blotted with Mary's tears, from her prayer book.

announcement was ever made, and no further public statement was issued about the Queen's pregnancy, though a great deal was said in private. It was the subject of coarse jokes in the taverns, and at secret Protestant prayer-meetings it was interpreted as a divine judgment on Mary. For the Queen, for the Spaniards and for loyal Catholics, it was a heavy blow.

The burning of the heretics had begun in February 1555. At the end of January a special commission, with Gardiner

Mary's letter to Cardinal Pole in May 1555 telling him of her pregnancy; many copies of this letter were prepared but never sent.

... right trusty and right entirely beloved Cousin we ...
... it hath pleased almighty god of his infinite goodness
... of other his benefits bestowed upon us, the gladding
... of a prince for the we do most humbly thank
... to be surely towards us as what soever shall
... same can not be but acceptable unto you also, we
... unto you this happy news of ours to content
... praying for us give god thanks for this his
... under our signet at our honour of Hampton court
... and second year of ours and my lord the

presiding, sat to try the case of Rogers, Hooper and others, and condemned them as heretics. On 4 February Rogers was burned at Smithfield. As the first martyr of Mary's reign, he earned the distinction, in Protestant eyes, of being the proto-martyr, as St Stephen had been during the first persecution of the Christians fifteen hundred years before. As Rogers was a married priest, Gardiner refused his request to be allowed to see his wife and children and say goodbye to them before he was burned, though this privilege was granted to all the martyrs except the married priests, and sometimes even to married priests by kindly gaolers who were prepared to disobey the orders which they had received from their superiors. But Rogers's wife and children, and many of his friends, came to Smithfield to see him burned, and made a demonstration in his support. When some pigeons were smoked out of their nests in the neighbouring houses, and flew over the fire in which Rogers was burning, some of the Protestants said that it marked the presence of the Holy Ghost.

Hooper was taken to Gloucester to be burned in his old diocese. When Mary signed the order for his execution, she directed that he was not to be allowed to address the onlookers before he was burned, as he would probably use the occasion to make Protestant propaganda. Hooper's burning was a particularly horrible one. It was usual for the authorities to permit the martyr to have a bag of gunpowder around his neck, so that when the flames touched the gunpowder it would explode and kill him instantly; but in Hooper's case the powder did not explode, and the fire burned badly. It took three-quarters of an hour, after the faggots were lit, for Hooper to die. Foxe compared Hooper to Polycarp, the early Christian martyr who was burned in the second century; but the Catholic writer Parsons could not understand the comparison, because 'St Polycarp was martyred by Jews and infidels', whereas Hooper 'was lawfully chastised by Christian superiors according to the ecclesiastical canons'.

In the course of the year, most of the Protestant bishops and leading theologians who had not escaped abroad were burned. Ferrar, the Bishop of St David's under Edward VI, was burned at Carmarthen in March 1555; and in October Ridley and Latimer were burned at Oxford, after being tried for a second time and condemned again as heretics, this time by a commission acting under the authority of Pole as Papal Legate. In Ridley's case, as in Hooper's, the fire burned slowly, and death was prolonged and very terrible. Apart from the four bishops, the victims included such prominent Protestants as Rowland Taylor, Bradford, Saunders and Philpot. The burnings continued for nearly four years, until Mary's death in November 1558. More than half the martyrs came from London, Kent and Essex. There were many in Norfolk, Suffolk and Sussex, and several in the Midlands, Gloucestershire and South Wales. There were none further north than Chester.

The martyrs came from all social classes except the nobility. Apart from the men who had been bishops and leading theologians under Edward VI, there were country gentlemen, merchants from the boroughs, and a large number of artisans and labouring men and women. The martyrs did not all hold the same views, and some of them held doctrines so extreme that they might have been burned as heretics by the Protestant bishops who were now suffering as their fellow-martyrs. The common danger and suffering which the martyrs faced did not make them forget their differences. When Philpot, the former Archdeacon of Winchester, was arrested as a heretic by Mary's officers and taken to the King's Bench prison in Southwark, he met another prisoner there who had been arrested as a heretic a few weeks earlier. This man held doctrines which were known as Arian, and denied the divinity of Christ, in which Philpot, like nearly all the Protestant martyrs, devoutly believed. When Philpot met the Arian in the King's Bench prison, he spat in his face. Some of his friends criticised Philpot for this, and thought that his behaviour to a fellow-prisoner had been un-Christian; but Philpot spent his time in prison, while he was waiting to be burned, in writing a treatise justifying his action, with the makeshift pencil and paper which he had managed to obtain secretly. The title of his treatise was 'An Apology of John Philpot written for spitting upon an Arian'. Both Philpot and the Arian were burned soon afterwards at Mary's orders.

The burning of the Protestant martyrs did great harm to the Catholic cause in which Mary believed so sincerely. For four hundred years after her death English and Irish Catholics continued to suffer some degree of persecution or victimisation,

171

largely because of the resentment aroused by her actions between 1555 and 1558. It is difficult to know how much of this hatred existed at the time, and how much arose during the next half-century as a result of the Protestant propaganda in Elizabeth's reign. The chief instrument in this propaganda was John Foxe, a Protestant priest from Lincolnshire, who was perhaps particularly eloquent on the subject of the persecution because he was one of the very few people in the sixteenth century who had at least some compunction about burning people with whose opinions he did not agree. During the reign of Edward VI, Foxe wrote a book about the Protestant martyrs who had suffered for their faith at the stake from the time of the Lollards in the fourteenth century to the death of Henry VIII; and he added an account of the sufferings of the early Christian martyrs under the Roman Caesars in order to associate them with the Protestant martyrs of his own age. He had nearly finished the book when Mary came to the throne, and he escaped abroad, taking his manuscript with him; and he expanded it to include a record of the martyrdoms of the Protestants – many of whom he knew personally – who were now suffering under Mary. When he returned to England after Mary's death, he published his completed work. Elizabeth's government ordered that a copy should be placed, along with the English Bible, in every cathedral and in many churches in the country, to remind the people of what happened under a Catholic Queen.

But there seems no doubt that, even before Elizabeth became Queen and Foxe wrote his book, there had been widespread anger at the burnings in south-eastern England, although thirty years before, in Henry VIII's reign, the people had quite happily accepted the burning of Protestant heretics as a very proper enforcement of the law of England. There were three reasons why they adopted a different attitude about the burnings in Mary's reign. In the first place, the scale of the executions was something quite new in England, though the number of Mary's victims was small compared with the executions carried out by King Philip in the Netherlands, and the hundred thousand massacred on both sides in the civil wars of religion in France. Henry VII burned ten heretics in twenty-four years. Henry VIII burned eighty-one in thirty-eight years, including one Catholic – the only Catholic who was ever burned for heresy in England.

172

Two Protestant extremists were burned during the six-year reign of Edward VI, and five by Elizabeth I during her forty-four years. Mary burned 283 in under four years – an average of one burning every five days between 4 February 1555 and 10 November 1558. (Other estimates give the number of Mary's victims as 273 and 277.) Another factor was the class and distinction of many of the martyrs. It was one thing to accept, in 1530, that cranky intellectual priests, or weird working-class soap-box preachers, were heretics who deserved to be burned for corrupting religion; but it was more difficult to believe that the man who yesterday was the bishop of the diocese, laying down the law about what religious doctrines were to be accepted, was today a heretic who must be burned. People became cynical about religion; they changed their religious views to further their interests and save their skins, and no longer accepted the moral authority of the ecclesiastical tribunals which condemned the heretics. Finally, there was the fact that the persecutions in Mary's reign were connected, in the people's minds, with the rule of a Spanish King and the supremacy of an Italian Pope.

It was very unfair of the people to blame the Spaniards for the persecution. Carranza, one of the Spanish priests who came with Philip, afterwards claimed that he was chiefly responsible for the burning of heretics in England in Mary's reign; but his statement is not reliable, because he made it in prison, after his return to Spain, where he was imprisoned for seventeen years on a charge of being sympathetic to heretics. Many of Philip's advisers tried to restrain the zeal of the persecutors. When the burnings began in February 1555, Renard wrote to the Emperor expressing his anxiety, because he knew that the English people would blame the Spaniards for it. He was worried by the demonstration which had occurred at Rogers's burning, and hoped that Philip would be able to restrain the zeal of Gardiner and the English bishops. In March 1555 Alphonso de Castro, one of Philip's Spanish chaplains, preached a sermon at Court which caused some stir. He condemned religious persecution, and said that heretics ought if possible to be won over by kindness, not sent to the stake. There is no record of what Mary thought of the sermon, but it did not make her relax the persecution. On one occasion she issued a proclamation urging

Foxe's Book of Martyrs

John Foxe (opposite) was already compiling a book of martyrs when Mary came to the throne. He fled to the Continent and completed his book with the sufferings of the Protestants under Mary. On Elizabeth's accession he returned to England and published his *Book of Martyrs* which was placed alongside Bibles in churches as a constant reminder of Mary's persecutions.

LEFT A line of
Protestant prisoners
being taken to trial
in London.

BELOW LEFT Bishop
Bonner, who was noted
for his cruelty, in
the act of 'scourgynge
of Goddes Saynctes in
his orchard'.

the bishops to burn only the worst offenders, and stated that
'especially within London I would wish none to be burned
without some of the Council's presence; and both there and
everywhere good sermons at the same'. But on several other
occasions she sent directives to the bishops urging them to show
more energy in suppressing heresy.

In later centuries, when the idea of religious persecution and
burning heretics had been rejected by everyone, historians argued
as to who was to blame for the savagery of the Marian persecution. At the time, the Protestants tended to blame Gardiner,
who had been the leader of the anti-Protestant faction at Court
under Henry VIII, and was now again most prominent in
instigating the persecution. Gardiner had always been an
authoritarian and a disciplinarian, and undoubtedly favoured
the policy of re-introducing the heresy laws, and burning the
men who had been the leaders of the Protestant Reformation
under Edward VI. But though Gardiner presided at the first
heresy trial in 1555, in order to lend his prestige and the authority
of his office as Lord Chancellor to the persecution, he afterwards
devoted his attention to foreign policy, and played a less active
part in burning heretics under Mary than he had done under
Henry VIII. In any case, he died in November 1555, and the
persecution continued for three years, and became more
terrible, after his death. Bonner, the Bishop of London, was
particularly hated by the Protestants because of his brutality
and coarse humour, and the fact that so many of the martyrs
came from his diocese, and were tried and sentenced by him;
but Bonner was never influential at Court, or responsible for
state policy. Cardinal Pole, under whose authority as Papal
Legate the heresy courts acted, played a part in the execution of
Cranmer; but even Foxe gives him credit for being a less savage
persecutor than most of the other persons in authority, and says
that he preferred digging up and burning the corpses of dead
heretics rather than burning live ones. Some of the most
enthusiastic persecutors were the leaders of the second rank –
younger men like Nicholas Harpsfield, the Archdeacon of
Canterbury, who still had their career to make. But there is no
doubt that the chief responsibility for the persecution lay with
Mary. Either the Wyatt rebellion, or some personal factor of
which we know nothing, caused a complete change in her

Coram Dno Rege et Dña Regina apud westm Termino Sci hillarij Annis Regnoz Philippi et marie Dei grā Regis et Regine Anglie hispaniaz franc

attitude, and destroyed all her merciful instincts which had been in evidence before. Mary was the only person in England who could have stopped the persecution at any time if she had wished to do so; and in fact the burnings stopped on the day when she died.

Mary introduced a new and terrible element into the persecution. Until now, it had been accepted in England that the object of heresy proceedings was to force the heretic to recant, and every effort was made, both at his trial and afterwards, to obtain a recantation. If all other attempts had failed, and the heretic was brought to the stake, it was the almost invariable practice, before the faggots were lit, to offer him a pardon if he would recant. The authorities realised that if a heretic recanted under these circumstances, his recantation would not necessarily be sincere, as he might have recanted only to avoid the fire; but they were satisfied if they could obtain from the heretic a public submission to the authority of the Church.

But this was not good enough for Mary. She was not satisfied with an insincere recantation. In January 1556 she took the unprecedented step of ordering that heretics should no longer be given an opportunity of recanting at the stake. She had been angered by the constancy with which the heretics, during the previous year, had refused the opportunity to save their lives by a recantation; and she directed the sheriffs that in view of the contempt with which her offer of pardon had been received by the heretics, the chance should not be offered to them in future.

This new severity was applied for the first time in Cranmer's case. Cranmer was burned despite the fact that he had recanted. The Protestant exiles abroad wrote a pamphlet, *A Supplication to the Queen's Majesty*, which they sent to Mary, reminding her that Cranmer had interceded for her life in 1536; but Mary refused to read Protestant literature. According to the Catholic writer Alan Cope, she refused to read a petition which Cranmer sent her. Cope wrote that when she received Cranmer's letter, she gave it to Pole, asking him 'whether she was permitted to read, or even to accept, a letter written by a heretic; so wise and holy was this woman in matters concerning the Catholic faith'.

Only a small number of Protestants were prepared to face martyrdom. One of the martyrs admitted, in a moment of frankness, that only ten per cent of the Protestants remained true to their principles. The great majority conformed, and went to Mass. They justified their apostasy by the convenient doctrine that it was their duty, as good Christians, to obey their sovereign and change their religion when the Queen ordered them to do so. But many people, though not prepared to be martyrs themselves, had great respect for those who were prepared to make the sacrifice, and they regarded the sufferers not as heretics on the road to Hell, but as martyrs on the road to Heaven. Many people came up to the heretics on their way to the stake and asked them for their blessing. In January 1556 Mary sent an indignant circular to the sheriffs of the counties complaining that the burning of a heretic, instead of being the edifying spectacle and impressive deterrent to heresy that it was supposed to be, was being turned into a demonstration in support of the heretics; and she ordered the sheriffs to arrest anyone who showed sympathy for a heretic at the stake. This order was only spasmodically enforced; but in the autumn of 1557 a man at Norwich, who protested against the agony suffered by a heretic in the fire, was arrested, put in the stocks, and flogged through the market with a dog-whip.

A number of Protestants, confronted with the choice of going to Mass or being burned, escaped abroad, and settled in the Protestant cities of Switzerland and Germany. At first, Mary does not seem to have tried very hard to prevent them from going. She did not issue them with passports to go, and as it was always illegal to leave the kingdom without a passport, the refugees went secretly and illegally, paying fishermen to take them from the port of London, or from Rye, to Emden or to Dieppe, where Henry II, in order to annoy Mary, did not arrest them and burn them, as he was burning the French Protestants. But Mary did not make any great effort to catch them as they escaped, or to prevent their friends and sympathisers in England from sending them money to maintain them in exile. At the request of the King of Denmark she allowed Coverdale, the Protestant Bishop of Exeter and translator of the Bible, to leave England with a passport and go to Denmark.

As the burning of the heretics got underway, Mary changed her attitude. Measures were taken to stop money being sent from England to the refugees abroad. Mary became almost as

The Pamphleteers

As printing became widespread and more efficient, books and pamphlets became a strong form of propaganda. Protestants who had escaped abroad were able to write unmolested and smuggle their work back to England. Chief among these was John Knox whose famous pamphlet against 'the monstrous regiment of women' (right) was written in Mary's reign but later directed against Mary, Queen of Scots.

THE FIRST
BLAST OF THE
TRVMPET AGAINST
THE MONSTRVOVS
regiment of
women.
❖

Veritas temporis
filia.

M. D. LVIII.

❡ To the mooste excellent
and vertuouse Queene, Ma-
rye by the grace of GOD,
Quene of England, Fraunce,
and Irelande, and Defendour
of the fayth, John Christofer-
son her graces Chapleyne, ¢
dayly oratour wissheth a long,
a quiete, and a prosperous
reygne with the daylye
encrease of al godly
vertue.

Lyke as there
be manye and
sondrye disea-
ses (most gra-
tious Soue-
raigne) which
chaunsing to a mans body, so
sore manye times trouble and
vexe the same, that they not
A.ij.   onlye

LEFT Not all the propaganda was on the Protestant side. In 1554 the Catholic J. Christopherson wrote this pamphlet as 'An Exhortation to all menne to take hede and beware of rebellion'.

Typographus. **Der Buchdrucker.**

ARte mea reliquas illustro Typographus artes,
  Imprimo dum varios ære micante libros.
Quæ prius aucta situ, quæ puluere plena iacebant,
  Vidimus obscura nocte sepulta premi.

Hæc veterum renouo neglecta volumina Patrum
  Atq; scolis curo publica facta legi.
Artem prima nouam reperisse Moguntia fertur,
  Vrbs grauis, & multis ingeniosa modis.
Qua nihil vtilius videt, aut preciosius orbis,
  Vix melius quicquam secla futura dabunt.

Concinnator librorum. **Buchbinder.**

QVisquis in Aonijs studiosus obambulat hortis,
  Et studijs tempus mitibus omne locat.
Huc properet, vigili ferat atq; volumina dextra,
  Edita Calcographus quæ prius ære dedit.

Hic ego campactos tibi leuigo ritè libellos,
  Et polio; picta post modo pelle tego.
Sericeis etiam ligis operosus adorno,
  Atq; comis, summa qua decet arte seco.
Inter vt Aonidum vel mille volumina pulchrè
  Emineat cultu conueniente liber.

A printer (left) and a bookbinder from Jost Amman's
illustrations to *Acceserunt* by Schopperius.

resentful as Henry VIII had been about the propaganda which was being carried on by the refugees, and she sent agents to spy on them. In 1556 Edward VI's Protestant tutor, Sir John Cheke, who had gone abroad when Mary became Queen, was kidnapped by Mary's agents while he was travelling in the Netherlands, and, with the consent of the Emperor's officers, was brought back to England. Cheke saved his life by recanting and becoming a Catholic, and promising to perform penance for having been a Protestant. The penance imposed was to compel him to sit on the bench beside the judge at heresy trials when his former Protestant colleagues were tried for heresy.

The doctrines of the English Protestants underwent an important change as a result of Mary's persecution. Hitherto they had accepted, as one of the central points of their faith, the duty of the Christian to obey the King, who would free them from the domination of the Pope and regulate the religion of his subjects. Many of the Protestants continued to hold this view even under Mary, and believed that though they must be ready to suffer martyrdom for their faith, they were not entitled to resist Mary's authority. But some of the younger Protestant leaders in exile put forward a new and revolutionary doctrine. On the basis of texts from the Old Testament, they argued that subjects had not only the right, but the duty, to resist wicked rulers.

These revolutionary opinions were put forward by three forceful Protestant pamphleteers. John Ponet, the former Bishop of Winchester, who had fled to Germany after fighting for Wyatt, wrote *A Short Treatise of Politic Power*. Christopher Goodman, an English refugee in Geneva, wrote *How Superior Powers ought to be obeyed*; and the Scot John Knox, who had come to England as a refugee from Scotland, but had escaped from England after Mary's accession and was also in Geneva, wrote several revolutionary pamphlets against Mary, of which the most sensational was his *First Blast of the Trumpet against the Monstrous Regiment of Women*. The *First Blast of the Trumpet*, which was later used as an argument against Mary Queen of Scots in Scotland, was directed chiefly against Mary Tudor when Knox wrote it in 1558.

These books, and other Protestant pamphlets, were printed abroad, but were smuggled into England and secretly distributed there, especially in London. Mary issued repeated proclamations against these seditious books. In 1558 she ordered that anyone found in possession of these books, who had not handed them over to the authorities, was to be put to death summarily, without trial, under martial law. She also ordered, from time to time, that copies of the books of heretical authors should be solemnly burned at a great public ceremony.

Ponet, in his book, used a forceful argument, which was probably as effective as any with the ordinary Englishman.

> When were ever things so dear in England as in this time of the Popish Mass and other idolatry restored? Whoever heard or read before that a pound of beef was at fourpence? A sheep twenty shillings. A pound of candles at fourpence. A pound of butter at fourpence. A pound of cheese at fourpence. Two eggs one penny; a quarter of wheat sixty-four shillings. A quarter of malt at one shilling or above; the people driven of hunger to grind acorns for bread meal, and to drink water instead of ale.

These commodities at fourpence a pound were certainly expensive at a time when the daily wage of the unskilled labourer had only risen from fourpence to sevenpence.

8 Calais 1555-8

WHEN RENARD FIRST SUGGESTED TO MARY that she should marry Philip, she told him that if she did, she would fall very much in love with him, as the Church expected a wife to do. She kept this promise. Philip, on his part, treated her with every consideration, and was apparently very fond of her, though she was no longer young and had lost any good looks which she may once have had. As was to be expected, rumours circulated that Philip was having love affairs with Mary's ladies-in-waiting. In view of his unpopularity in England, it is not surprising that most of the stories about him were discreditable. He was said to have forced his attentions on Magdalen Dacre, one of Mary's ladies, and to have become so objectionable that she hit him over the head with a thick staff. This was almost certainly just spiteful gossip by political opponents.

In October 1555 Charles v abdicated, and retired to a life of luxury in a Spanish monastery. He handed over his territories in Germany and Austria, and his title of Holy Roman Emperor, to his brother Ferdinand, and left his more valuable possessions of Spain, with the American colonies, and the Netherlands to Philip, to whom he had already given the kingdom of Naples. This made it necessary for Philip to leave England in August 1555.

Mary was very sad that Philip had to leave her. She managed to preserve her queenly dignity as she took leave of him and his gentlemen-in-waiting at the head of the great staircase in the palace at Greenwich. Then she retired to a window in the gallery from which she could see Philip enter his barge; and, thinking that no one could see her, she wept bitterly as she waved to Philip and he waved most affectionately to her. He had hardly left before she wrote him a letter, and sent a messenger to catch him at Canterbury and deliver the letter to him. She wrote him several other letters while he was at Canterbury, which were carried by horsemen who, at Mary's orders, were kept always ready, with their horses saddled, in the palace courtyard.

The English chroniclers in later years, who had no good word to say for Philip, were determined to criticise him as much for going as for coming in the first place, and accused him of callously deserting Mary; but this is unfair, because he had to visit and govern his other kingdoms as well as England. He

PREVIOUS PAGES A scene from Moulet's engravings of the fall of Calais.

188

regarded England as one of his most important possessions, and until Mary died he was always referred to throughout Europe as 'the King of England'.

Mary had never been gay by temperament, and her Court became more solemn after Philip's departure. She had revived the splendour of Court life as it had existed at the time of Henry VIII, after the rather puritanical simplicity of Edward VI's Court; but though foreign ambassadors commented on the rich quality and expensive material of Mary's dresses, and the quantity and value of her jewellery and of the decorations and ornaments of her Court, they also mentioned how sombre it was, with no sign of any bright colours anywhere, so that it almost gave the impression of being a Court in permanent mourning.

Mary was forty in 1556. Men and women of forty were older in the sixteenth century than they are today, but Mary was considered even by her contemporaries to be unusually old at forty. Her face was heavily wrinkled, though the Venetian ambassador thought that this was caused by anxiety, not by age or poor health. Her complexion was still agreeable, being very pink and white; her voice was low and masculine, as it had always been; and she was more bony and skinny than ever. She had become very short-sighted, and was in the habit of staring at people with a piercing glance that was sometimes a little frightening. The Venetian ambassador wrote that no one could despise her for being ugly without admiring her dignity as a Queen.

She worked very hard, and led an abstemious life. She rose early in the morning – this probably means at five or six o'clock – and worked all the morning with her secretaries and her Council; but she did not eat a meal until 1 p.m. At night she never had more than three or four hours' sleep, because when she had finished all her official engagements and State business, she would sit up late at night writing to Philip. According to the French Ambassador, Noailles, she spent the rest of the night weeping, sighing and raging against her subjects. He was told by his informant that she sometimes had such vivid dreams during the night about her love and passion that she completely lost control of herself.

She was very regular in observing the feasts and fasts of the

OVERLEAF Mary exercises her mystic royal power: LEFT praying for blessing on rings which cure cramp; RIGHT touching a sufferer to cure the King's Evil.

Church and the canonical hours, attending Mass nine times a day, as everyone was supposed to do in theory, but which few people did. She was far more sincerely and deeply religious than most of her fellow-sovereigns. When she attended the great public ceremonies of the Church, such as the Creeping to the Cross on Good Friday at Greenwich in 1556, the courtiers and ambassadors were impressed, but also a little disconcerted, by the extraordinary emotion which she displayed. It was very different from the devout but restrained manner in which other Catholic kings and queens behaved on such occasions. She kissed the sores of twenty men and twenty women, who were suffering from scrofulous disease, with passionate enthusiasm.

Mary was admired and loved by her immediate entourage at Court. All her ladies-in-waiting were devoted to her. She probably had a more sensitive conscience than any of the other Tudor sovereigns, and this conscience, which was partly responsible for her cruelty to her religious opponents, made her a kind mistress to her servants and lovable in private life. She had none of her father's selfishness and his remarkable capacity to convince himself that his first duty to his kingdom and his people was to ensure his own safety, comfort and pleasure.

Out of consideration for her subjects, she did not travel around south-eastern England on a 'progress' in the summer, like the other Tudor sovereigns. She thought that these progresses caused too much inconvenience to the people, as it involved the requisitioning of carts and waggons when they were needed for haymaking and the harvest; and though she moved between her palaces of Whitehall, St James's, Greenwich and Hampton Court, to which she would normally travel by barge, she did not often go further afield. But her consideration for her subjects may not have been the only reason why Mary did not go on progresses; she knew that she had become very unpopular, and her advisers may have feared for her safety on the journey. When she rode through London with Philip on 26 August 1555 on their way to Greenwich, before Philip left England, many men did not take off their hats to the King and Queen, or to the cross that was carried before them; and Gardiner, who was riding with them, ordered his secretary to make a note of the houses where the people did not salute.

Mary's courtiers were touched by her almost childlike

simplicity in certain ways, though in public and political matters she often showed great shrewdness. One example of her naïveté was her ignorance of the ways of the world in sexual matters, and of coarse words which were in common use at her Court. One day the Lord Chamberlain, Lord William Howard, was leaving Mary's presence after an audience, when he met Mrs Frances Neville, one of Mary's ladies, in the Queen's ante-chamber. Lord William tickled Frances under her chin as he passed, and said gaily to her: 'My pretty whore, how dost thou?' Mary overheard what he said, but she did not know what the word 'whore' meant. A few minutes later, she called Frances Neville into her chamber and asked her to adjust her dress, the great farthingale skirt of the period. As Frances knelt at her feet, fixing the farthingale, Mary said to her 'God-a-mercy, my pretty whore.' Frances was overcome with embarrassment, and told the Queen how deeply distressed she was to hear Her Majesty call her by such a name. Mary said that she had heard the Lord Chamberlain call Frances by the same name. Frances explained: 'My Lord Chamberlain is an idle gentleman, and we respect not what he saith or doth; but Your Majesty, from whom I think never any heard such a word, doth amaze me either in jest or earnest to be called so by you. A whore is a wicked, misliving woman.' Mary assured Frances that she had not intended to make any aspersions on her moral character, as she had never heard the word 'whore' before.★

Mary still went out walking in the country near her various houses, and often took the opportunity to visit the people in their cottages. On these occasions, she was usually accompanied by only one lady, and was often unrecognised. This idea of a sovereign visiting his lowliest subjects in their homes was found in many of the medieval legends, but it was unusual for sixteenth-

★This story was told by Mary's lady-in-waiting, Jane Dormer, Duchess of Feria, shortly before her death in 1612, to her servant, Henry Clifford, and recorded by him in his manuscript *Life of Jane Dormer, Duchess of Feria*, which he wrote in 1643. When Clifford's manuscript was published by Burns and Oates in London in 1887, the word 'whore' was not printed, but was replaced by an asterisk; the editor, the Reverend Joseph Stevenson, explaining in a footnote: 'The expression here used will not bear repetition'. An examination of Clifford's manuscript, which is in the possession of Lord Dormer at Grove Park, shows that the suppressed word was 'whore'.

A woman spinning in her
cottage. Mary liked to
visit the common people
on the royal estates.

194

century sovereigns to do this. On one occasion Mary called at the cottage of a poor carter who did not know who Mary was, but in the course of the conversation told Mary how he had been swindled by one of her petty officials who had refused to pay him what was owed him for bringing coal to the palace. When Mary returned home she ordered the matter to be investigated, and saw to it that justice was done to the carter.

It was typical of Mary's character and outlook that her concern for her people's welfare was expressed on the personal, and not on the political, level. Though she visited the poor in their cottages, she did not introduce any legislation to deal with the social and economic evils which caused so much discontent. She made no attempt, like Somerset, to solve the problems created by enclosures of common land, and by inflation, probably because all her energies in internal politics were devoted to the suppression of heresy. She believed that it was more important to ensure the spiritual welfare of her subjects by burning heretics than to provide for their economic welfare; and she could not afford to antagonise the nobility, gentry and merchant classes who sat in Parliament by interfering with enclosures and speculators' profits, if she wanted their support for the suppression of heresy, the Spanish marriage and the reunion with Rome. The only statute dealing with enclosures which was passed in her reign was an Act which increased the rigour of Northumberland's statute of 1549, making it an offence punishable by death to break down a fence surrounding enclosed land.

Mary took an interest in the development of English commerce. It was during her reign that diplomatic and trade relations with Russia were first established. A few weeks before Edward VI died, two English sea-captains, Willoughby and Chancellor, sailed from London on a voyage of discovery to find the north-east sea passage to China. They did not find it, but discovered the way to the White Sea, which was the only sea-route to Russia, as Russian territory did not yet reach to the Baltic or the Black Sea. Willoughby was frozen to death in the Arctic, but Chancellor reached Moscow, where he was well received by the young Tsar, Ivan the Terrible. Two years later he returned from a second visit with Ivan's Ambassador, Oseph Nepea. They sailed from the mouth of the Dvina in July 1556,

Trade with Russia

The need to find new markets for the export of
woollen cloth, and the lure of fabled riches of
the Orient, led to the formation of the Merchant
Adventurers' Company in 1552, with the aim of
finding a north-east passage to China and Japan.
One of the leaders, Chancellor, succeeded
instead in reaching Moscow, where he found
Ivan the Terrible wearing 'a long garment of
beaten gold' and carrying 'a staff of crystal and
gold'. The Tsar was anxious to open trade with
England, and Chancellor returned to England
to bring letters from Mary and Philip
concluding a trade agreement. The Merchant
Adventurers were granted a monopoly of the
Russian trade and re-formed as the Moscovy
Company.

RIGHT A Russian merchant of 1560 from
Trachtenbuch by Hans Wiegel.

Engravings from
Chancellor's
description of
his voyage.
LEFT Russian cavalry.
RIGHT Cavalry saddles
and equipment.

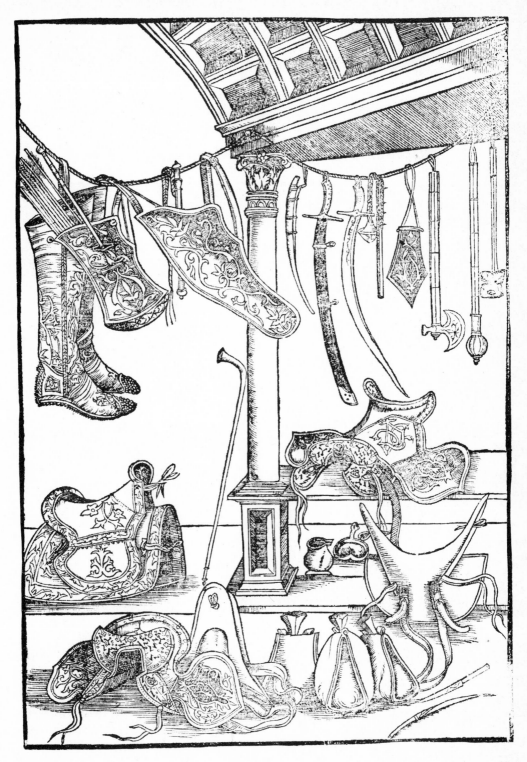

but were wrecked off the coast of Scotland, where Chancellor was drowned in saving Nepea's life; and Nepea did not reach London till February 1557. He was received in audience by Mary, and they signed a treaty under which an English trading colony was allowed to settle at Archangel to develop commercial relations between England and Russia.

In 1555 Pope Julius III died. Mary hoped that Pole might be chosen as the new Pope, and she and Philip and Charles V used their influence in Rome on his behalf; but Cardinal Cervini was chosen, and became Pope Marcellus II. He reigned for a shorter time than any other Pope in history, and died twenty-one days after his election, on 30 April 1555. In the new Conclave, Mary and the Emperor renewed their efforts on Pole's behalf, but the French agents worked for Cardinal Caraffa. Charles V made it clear to the Conclave that he would not agree to the selection of Caraffa, using the so-called imperial veto, which had no legal standing, but was always observed in practice; but the French scored a great diplomatic triumph, and Caraffa was chosen as Pope Paul IV. For the first time in many years, the Pope was pro-French and anti-Habsburg.

Paul IV was seventy-nine when he became Pope; he had been the Papal Nuncio in London before Mary was born. Serious allegations about his private character were made by his contemporaries; but these may have been slanders put around by the agents of Charles V and Philip of Spain. They said that he was always drunk, or, alternatively, that he was mad. These are probably exaggerations, though it is certainly true that he had a great appetite for eating and drinking, and was liable to have outbursts of hysterical rage.

Paul IV had one great object – to drive the Habsburgs out of Italy. In the autumn of 1556 a secret report from one of Philip's agents on the weakness of the military defences of the Papal States fell into the Pope's hands, and Paul treated it as a threat to the Holy See. Philip was very reluctant to quarrel with the Pope, and made every effort to avoid a rupture; but this only encouraged the Pope to adopt a provocative attitude, and he and Henry II of France were determined to go to war with Philip. The Pope drafted a bull excommunicating Philip and Charles V; but Philip expelled the Papal Nuncio from Spain, and prohibited any of his Spanish subjects, on pain of death, from publishing

OPPOSITE Pope Paul IV receiving the Venetian Ambassador.

198

the papal censures in his territories, or from going to Rome. The Pope then issued a bull which deprived Philip of his kingdom of Naples, and called in French troops to protect the Papal States. Philip ordered his armies in Naples to invade the papal territories. He declared that he was acting with the greatest reluctance, like a dutiful son who attempts to snatch the knife from his father's hand when he sees him brandishing it in a fit of temporary insanity. Philip's method of 'snatching the knife' was to authorise the Duke of Alva, his general, to sack the papal towns that he captured and hang the garrison.

Mary was greatly upset by this quarrel between her husband and the Holy Father; but although Paul IV did not take any action against Mary herself, she was drawn into the war which split Catholic Europe. England came in on Philip's side against France and the Pope. When Mary, in the traditional manner, sent a herald to the French Court to issue a formal challenge and declaration of war to Henry II, Henry's reaction showed how the idea of a woman ruler had still not been completely accepted in Europe. He burst out laughing, and said: 'Consider how I stand when a woman challenges me to war.' Some of the English Protestant refugees in France offered their services to Henry II; they were as ready to commit high treason from ideological motives as were some of the English Catholics in the reigns of Henry VIII and Elizabeth I. The French sent forty English Protestants under Thomas Stafford, who was Cardinal Pole's nephew, to start a rebellion in Yorkshire. They captured Scarborough, but were defeated, captured and executed.

Mary prepared to send English troops to help Philip in Europe; but she was very distressed at being forced to take sides against the Pope. Pole tried to help. He wrote a series of letters to Philip and the Pope urging the need for reconciliation, as only the heretics would benefit from the present situation. But he succeeded only in angering both Philip and Paul. The Pope replied by accusing Pole of heresy, and of having been soft towards heretics ten years before when he was the papal governor of Viterbo. He deprived Pole of his office of Papal Legate in England, and recalled him to Rome to answer the charges against him. Mary begged Paul to revoke this order, because it would do incalculable harm if Pole were recalled and disgraced so soon after England had submitted to papal

200

supremacy through Pole's agency; but the Pope rejected her plea, and appointed Friar Peto to succeed Pole as Legate.

Peto had been Mary's confessor when she was a child. At that time he had been at the Greyfriars monastery at Greenwich; but he had gone abroad after denouncing the divorce proceedings against Catherine of Aragon in a sermon in Henry VIII's presence in 1532. After living in exile for twenty-two years, and being condemned as a traitor in his absence, he had returned to Greenwich when Mary restored the Greyfriars monastery there, and was peaceably spending his last days there. The Spanish statesman Count Figueroa described Peto as 'a man over eighty and of no ability whatever, but a good man, and a Christian, who recognises his own shortcomings'.

In June 1557 the Pope suddenly made Peto a Cardinal. Peto, realising that this was a prelude to his appointment as Legate instead of Pole, refused; but on 20 June Paul wrote to Mary that he had appointed Peto as Legate in Pole's place, and that he was recalling Pole to Rome. Mary's ambassador in Rome told her that if Pole came to Rome he would be immediately arrested as a heretic. Mary refused to permit Pole to go to Rome. When the Papal Nuncio arrived at Calais, bearing the Pope's order appointing Peto as Legate and recalling Pole to Rome, he was informed by the English officials there that Mary would not permit him to set foot in England, and he was ordered to leave English territory at once.

Paul's furious denunciations were useless against Philip's army. Alva and his troops marched to Rome, and forced Paul to make peace. The prestige of the Pope's office was enough to ensure that even in this situation he was treated with respect. Philip ordered Alva to kneel at the Pope's feet and implore his pardon for having invaded his territories; but the Pope had to accept the peace terms which Philip dictated.

In March 1557 Philip returned to England, but not for long. He had come to make preparations for the invasion of France, which he was planning to launch in the summer from his territories in the Netherlands with a combined army of Spanish and English troops. After staying in England for four months, he left in July, and invaded France with an army of forty thousand men. He marched on St Quentin, which was held by a French garrison commanded by Admiral Coligny, who later

became one of the leaders of the Protestants in the French civil war, and was killed in the massacre of St Bartholomew. Philip besieged St Quentin, and a French army marched to the relief of the town. On St Lawrence's Day, 10 August 1557, a battle was fought outside the walls of St Quentin. The Spanish and English army, who outnumbered the French by nearly four to one, won a great victory; the French lost three thousand men killed and five thousand taken prisoner, while Philip's losses were negligible. A fortnight later, Philip captured St Quentin by assault; Coligny, who was wounded, was taken prisoner. It was a great triumph for the King of England, and Mary and the government propagandists tried to make the English people proud of him. But the people would not think of Philip as another Henry V, and of St Quentin as a second Agincourt; and four months later, England suffered a loss which completely overshadowed the glory of St Quentin.

For two hundred years England had held the Marches of Calais, which consisted of the town of Calais, the fortress of Guisnes and a strip of territory about twenty-five miles long and running inland for a depth of six miles from the coast. The English kept a permanent garrison in the Marches, under the command of the Deputy of Calais, Lord Wentworth; and in wartime the size of the garrison had been increased. The English were not expecting to be attacked in Calais because it was unusual in the sixteenth century for armies to fight in the winter, when they usually withdrew into winter quarters and prepared for next summer's campaign; but on 22 December 1557 Lord Grey, the English commander in Guisnes, heard a rumour that the French were going to attack, and warned the Privy Council in London that he had not enough men to hold the territory against a strong enemy force.

The French army was commanded by Francis of Lorraine, Duke of Guise, the head of the family in eastern France which in one generation had risen to become one of the most powerful political forces in Europe. Five of Guise's brothers held high office in Church and State in France, and a sister was Queen Regent of Scotland and mother of Mary Queen of Scots. Guise was the best general in France, and afterwards became leader of the Catholics in the French civil war.

Guise and his army invaded the Marches of Calais on 31

OPPOSITE The battle of St Quentin during Philip's campaign in the Netherlands.

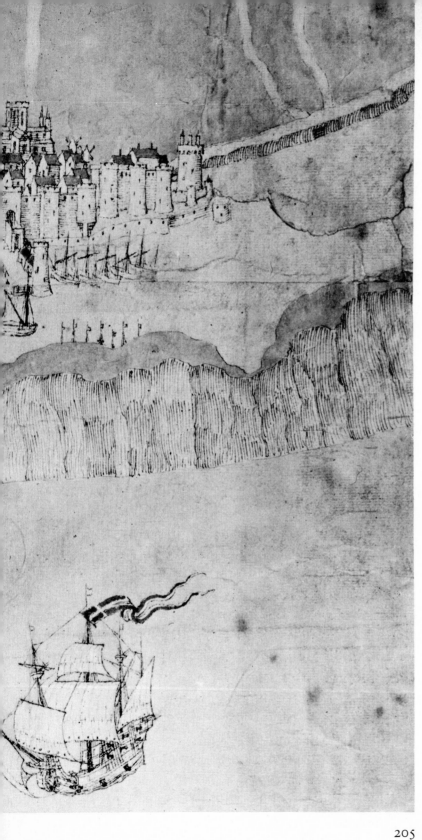

The port of Calais was
the last English-held
territory in France.

Henry II of France on a
medal commemorating
the fall of Calais.

December. There was a Spanish army at Gravelines, in Philip's
territory in the Netherlands, less than twenty miles from
Calais; and the English in Calais expected that their Spanish
allies would come to their assistance. But within three days
Guise had overrun the whole of the English territory except the
town of Calais and the fortress of Guisnes. On 2 January Mary
wrote to Wentworth to tell him that she was sending the Earl of
Rutland with reinforcements to Calais; but by 7 January Calais

206

had fallen to a French assault, and Guisnes surrendered a fortnight later.

The disaster led to bitter recriminations between the allies. Philip, who realised that the Spaniards would be blamed for the fall of Calais, bitterly reproached the English for its loss, which he said had seriously upset his military calculations. He said that he had warned Lord Wentworth, some weeks before, that the French were likely to attack the town, but that the English government had taken no steps to send reinforcements to Calais until it was too late. The Council in London threw all the blame on Wentworth, who had written to them on 29 December that he had sufficient forces to hold the town of Calais. This ignored the fact that Lord Grey had written as early as 22 December to tell them that the Marches were threatened and that reinforcements were needed; but both Wentworth and Grey had been taken prisoner by the French, and could not give their side of the story. Mary was very distressed at the loss of Calais and at Philip's reproaches; she was ashamed that the English had let Philip down. She ordered that Lord Wentworth should be charged with high treason for having 'adhered to the French King' on 29 December 1557; and all his property was seized while he was a prisoner of war in France. When he returned to England after the end of the war, in Elizabeth's reign, he was put on trial for treason, and acquitted.

In July 1558 the Spanish army under Egmont won a victory over the French at Gravelines; but the Spaniards made no attempt to follow up the victory by recapturing Calais. When peace was made next year, after Mary's death, England had to give up Calais, and never recovered it.

In the spring of 1558 Mary fell seriously ill. An epidemic of diseases, which the physicians of the period could not diagnose, was spreading through England, causing a very high death-rate throughout the country. The Protestants naturally interpreted it as a plague sent by God to punish the realm for Mary's sins. Mary herself seems to have suffered from dropsy, and her illness was made worse by her extreme melancholia. She spent a great deal of time weeping. She was unhappy that Philip was not there. She was unhappy about the loss of Calais. She was disturbed that her policy of suppressing heresy had not been more successful, that so many secret Protestant prayer-meetings were still taking place, and that heretical and seditious books were circulating in London.

The demonstrations in favour of the martyrs at the stake were becoming more and more daring. When seven heretics were burned at Smithfield on 7 June 1558, a large crowd cheered them enthusiastically, though Mary's proclamation against showing sympathy for heretics had been read out by the officials a few minutes earlier. Next month there was a more serious incident when a Protestant named Bembridge was burned at Winchester. The fire had been badly laid, and burned slowly; and after Bembridge's legs and face had been scorched, he cried out that he was ready to recant. The crowd called on the Sheriff of Hampshire, Sir Richard Pexall, to pardon Bembridge; and when he refused, the crowd ran to the stake, scattered the burning faggots, and carried the half-burned Bembridge out of the flames. Pexall then suspended the execution, and ordered that Bembridge be taken back to prison. On 1 August the Privy Council wrote to Pexall that the Queen thought it very strange that he had spared Bembridge, and that Bembridge was to be taken to the stake a second time and burned immediately. If Bembridge still adhered to the Catholic faith, as he pretended to do, a priest was to be present at his execution, 'for the better aiding of him to die God's servant'. Pexall was ordered to come before the Council at Richmond to explain his conduct. Mary imprisoned him for a short time, and then released him.

Above all, Mary was unhappy at the prospect of what would happen when Elizabeth became Queen. After Philip's second visit to England in the summer of 1557, Mary had again believed that she was pregnant; but again she was mistaken, and after everyone at Court had pretended, for several months, to believe that the birth of an heir was imminent, Mary realised that she was not going to have a child.

Elizabeth had returned to Court in April 1555. Before Philip left England for the first time, he had insisted that Mary should treat her as an honoured and affectionate sister. The Emperor and Renard had hoped, a year before, to settle the problem of Elizabeth effectively by cutting off her head; but that opportunity had been lost, and they had now come to accept that, as Mary was not going to have a child, it was inevitable that Elizabeth should succeed to the throne. The only thing to do was to bring her to Court and to try to win her goodwill. Philip treated her with much courtesy, and showed her so much attention, that the rumour went around that he was in love with her; but he was probably merely treating her with the gallantry which a prince ought to show to a princess.

In the summer of 1558 Philip wrote to his ambassador in England, the Count of Feria, and ordered him to go out of his way to ingratiate himself with Elizabeth. Philip realised that Mary might not have long to live, and was thinking of the possibility of marrying Elizabeth after Mary's death, and thus continuing to be King of England, provided that he could induce Paul IV to give the necessary dispensation for him to marry his deceased wife's sister. When Mary died, he did in fact propose marriage to Elizabeth, but she declined the offer. Mary was hurt when she heard about Philip's instructions to Feria; and Feria himself was unhappy about the position. He was about to marry Jane Dormer, one of Mary's ladies-in-waiting, who had always been a devoted Catholic; and, perhaps because of this, he was more alarmed than most other Spaniards at the danger of England becoming Protestant again. After Elizabeth became Queen, he and his wife went to Spain, where their home became a place of hospitality for English Catholic refugees; and Feria tried unsuccessfully to persuade Philip, in the early years of Elizabeth's reign, to adopt a tough policy towards England while it was still possible to do so.

Elizabeth had been regularly attending Mass since her return to Court, and was not showing the slightest sign of opposition to Mary's policy. But Mary was very suspicious of her, and was sure that she was a secret Protestant. Most of the Protestants thought so too, and were praying for her safety and for the day when she would become Queen. Mary considered the possibility of passing an Act of Parliament to alter Henry VIII's Will and exclude Elizabeth from the throne; but Philip would not hear of it. He knew that if Paget and his supporters in the Council, and the peers and members of the House of Commons, were unwilling to agree to this in 1554, there was no question of persuading them to do so now; and even if it were possible to exclude Elizabeth, it would be undesirable from the Spanish point of view. If Elizabeth were excluded, the next in line of succession was Mary Queen of Scots, Guise's niece, who had

been living at the French Court for the last ten years, and had just married the French Dauphin, and would soon be Queen of France. Philip preferred to see England ruled by a Protestant Queen than by a French Queen; and if Mary Queen of Scots were again excluded by the new Act of Parliament, this left only the Countess of Lennox and the sisters of Lady Jane Grey. Philip thought that if any of these became Queen, their authority would not be recognised, and that there would be a civil war in England which would give France the opportunity to intervene and take over the country.

In the summer of 1558, Philip wrote to Mary and asked her to give her jewels to Elizabeth, and in other ways to make a public gesture to show that she wished Elizabeth to succeed her as Queen. Mary complied with the greatest misgivings. She asked Elizabeth to promise that when she became Queen she would uphold the Catholic religion in England. Elizabeth promised to do so, but Mary did not believe her. Many of Mary's Councillors and courtiers visited Elizabeth at Hatfield, and seemed to spend more time there than at Court.

In October Mary heard that Charles V had died in his Spanish monastery. Although she had not seen him since she was a child of six, she was very sad when she heard the news, which distressed her more than could have been expected. Three weeks later she heard that Charles's sister, Mary of Hungary, who had been his regent in the Netherlands for many years, had also died. All the champions of the Catholic Church in Europe seemed to be going in the autumn of 1558. By the middle of November, Mary was sinking rapidly. At the same time, Cardinal Pole was dying at Lambeth Palace, and he and Mary at Whitehall sent messages to each other. Mary spent much time weeping. Her devoted ladies tried to comfort her, but she was so unhappy that she seemed to be dying of a broken heart.

Holinshed was told the reason by Mary's lady-in-waiting Mrs Rise, and twenty years later wrote about it in his *Chronicles of England, Scotland and Ireland*. Her Privy Councillors asked her why she was so sad, and said that they feared

> … that she took some thought for the King's Majesty her husband, which was gone from her. To whom she answering again: Indeed (said she) that may be one cause, but that is not the greatest wound

OPPOSITE Lady Jane Dormer by Antonio Moro. She was lady-in-waiting to Mary and married the Spanish ambassador, the Count of Feria. After Mary's death they returned to Spain and opened their house to Catholic refugees.

PLVS
VLTRA

MEDIOLANO
VINDICATO.

Successus neque te Cæsar spes certa petiti, Destituit, donec de littore
soluit Ibero, Neptuno sternente viam, Tritonibus Vdis, &c.

MARE
PACA
TO.

TREMIS=
SENO
RESTI=
TVTO.

SOLYMA=
NO.
PROFLIGA
TO.

ORBE
NOVO
INVE=
NTO.

An allegorical engraving made in
1559 of the death-ship of Charles v,
following the tradition of the ships
which bore the Celtic heroes to the
Isles of the Blessed.

212

that pierceth mine oppressed mind; but what that was she would not express to them. Albeit afterward she opened the matter more plainly to Mistress Rise and Mistress Clarentius (if it be true that they told me, which heard it of Mistress Rise herself), who then being most familiar with her, and most bold about her, told her that they feared she took thought for King Philip's departing from her. Not only that (said she) but when I am dead and opened, you will find Calais lying in my heart.

On 10 November five heretics were burned at Canterbury; they were the last to be executed in Mary's reign. Three days later, Mary signed the order for the burning of two London Protestants; but there was no time to carry out the order, and the two men died peacefully in their beds many years later.

On 17 November – a day which was to be celebrated every year by English Protestants for more than a century as Queen Elizabeth's Accession Day – Mary died at 4 a.m. She called all her ladies to her, and urged them always to remain steadfast in the Catholic faith. Then her priest celebrated Mass in her chamber. At the moment of the consecration of the Host, Mary gave a spasm of emotion, and hung her head and died. Thirty-six hours later, Cardinal Pole died.

Mary had agreed that Edward VI should have a Protestant funeral, and Elizabeth gave Mary a Catholic one. She was buried in Westminster Abbey on 14 December, with great pomp and the full Catholic ceremonial. The sermon was preached by John White, who had succeeded Gardiner as Bishop of Winchester, and had presided at several heresy trials in Mary's reign. His sermon was a long eulogy of Mary for her virtues and her devotion to the Church. One passage in the sermon was interpreted as being a criticism of Elizabeth, and he was placed under house arrest.

In her Will, Mary left legacies to the monasteries that she had restored, and to other charitable institutions. She left £1,000 to Pole. She asked that her mother's body should be moved from Peterborough Cathedral and buried beside her in Westminster Abbey; they had been forcibly separated in life, but she wished their bodies to be united in death. Elizabeth did not carry out these provisions in the Will. It would have been politically inexpedient to do so.

For a few weeks Elizabeth made no move about religion, but

THE ROSE IS RED THE LEAVES ARE GRENE GOD SAVE ELIZABETH OVR QVENE

1603

no one had any doubts as to what her policy would be. Early next year, William Cecil, whom she had appointed Secretary of State, drew up a paper in which he summarised, very clearly and succinctly, the advantages and disadvantages of England either remaining Catholic or becoming Protestant. On balance, he advised Elizabeth to adopt the more daring course and make England Protestant. She followed his advice.

Mary Tudor was by nature kind and considerate, and she showed these qualities in her private life and in her treatment of her servants, her ladies and the poor folk in the cottages at her

ABOVE A Lambeth Delft dish inscribed Elizabeth I.

OPPOSITE The celebrations in London on the arrival of Elizabeth.

215

gates. But, like nearly everyone else in the sixteenth century, she believed that it was her duty to burn alive anyone who held religious opinions which were more radical and unorthodox than her own. Most other rulers of the period, being less sincere and conscientious than Mary, often allowed themselves to be deflected from this duty by considerations of foreign policy, for reasons of expediency and out of personal friendships. But Mary did not, and was therefore a cruel persecutor even by the standards of her own time. Her policy of bringing back the papal authority, and her marriage to a Spanish prince, aroused the nationalistic prejudices and xenophobia of the English people; she failed completely to deal with inflation and rising food prices; she involved England in an unsuccessful war and lost Calais; and the co-religionists and personal friends of her victims came to power after her death and gained control of the means of propaganda. For these reasons, her name was remembered with horror by many generations of Englishmen.

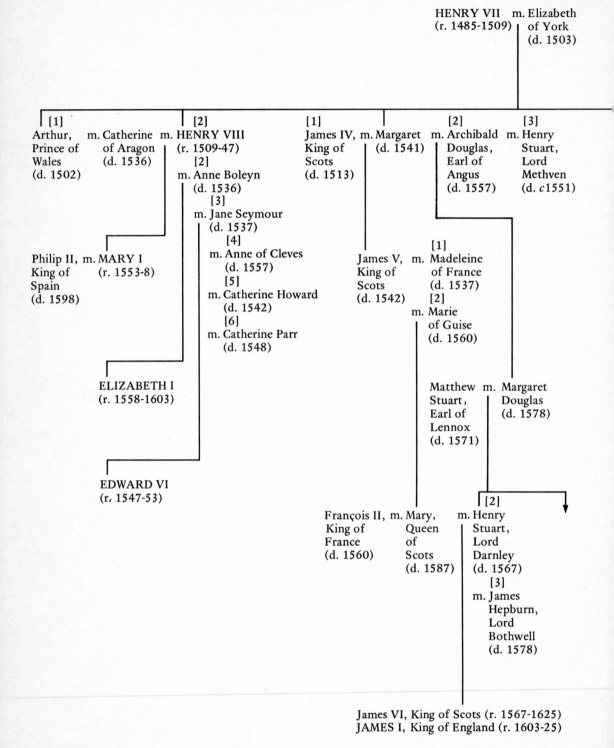

HENRY VII   m. Elizabeth
(r. 1485-1509)   of York
                     (d. 1503)

[1]   [2]   [1]   [2]   [3]
Arthur,   m. Catherine   m. HENRY VIII   James IV, m. Margaret   m. Archibald   m. Henry
Prince of   of Aragon   (r. 1509-47)   King of   (d. 1541)   Douglas,   Stuart,
Wales   (d. 1536)   [2]   Scots   Earl of   Lord
(d. 1502)   m. Anne Boleyn   (d. 1513)   Angus   Methven
                               (d. 1536)   (d. 1557)   (d. c1551)
                               [3]
                           m. Jane Seymour
                               (d. 1537)
                               [4]   [1]
Philip II, m. MARY I   m. Anne of Cleves   James V, m. Madeleine
King of   (r. 1553-8)   (d. 1557)   King of   of France
Spain   [5]   Scots   (d. 1537)
(d. 1598)   m. Catherine Howard   (d. 1542)   [2]
                               (d. 1542)   m. Marie
                               [6]   of Guise
                           m. Catherine Parr   (d. 1560)
                               (d. 1548)

                                                              Matthew m. Margaret
                                                              Stuart,   Douglas
                    ELIZABETH I   Earl of   (d. 1578)
                    (r. 1558-1603)   Lennox
                                                              (d. 1571)

                                                                                         [2]
                                          François II, m. Mary,   m. Henry
                    EDWARD VI   King of   Queen   Stuart,
                    (r. 1547-53)   France   of   Lord
                                          (d. 1560)   Scots   Darnley
                                                          (d. 1587)   (d. 1567)
                                                                           [3]
                                                                       m. James
                                                                           Hepburn,
                                                                           Lord
                                                                           Bothwell
                                                                           (d. 1578)

                              James VI, King of Scots (r. 1567-1625)
                              JAMES I, King of England (r. 1603-25)

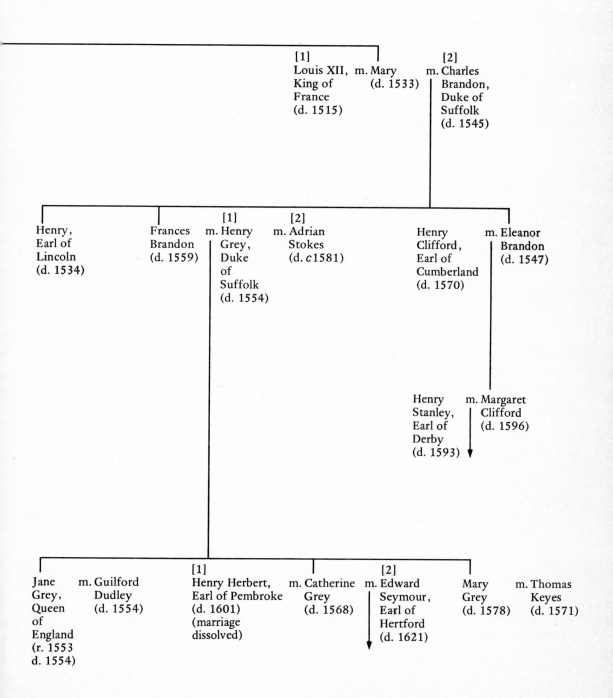

[1]
Louis XII, m. Mary
King of   (d. 1533)
France
(d. 1515)

[2]
m. Charles
Brandon,
Duke of
Suffolk
(d. 1545)

Henry,
Earl of
Lincoln
(d. 1534)

Frances
Brandon
(d. 1559)

[1]
m. Henry
Grey,
Duke
of
Suffolk
(d. 1554)

[2]
m. Adrian
Stokes
(d. c1581)

Henry
Clifford,
Earl of
Cumberland
(d. 1570)

m. Eleanor
Brandon
(d. 1547)

Henry
Stanley,
Earl of
Derby
(d. 1593)

m. Margaret
Clifford
(d. 1596)

Jane
Grey,
Queen
of
England
(r. 1553
d. 1554)

m. Guilford
Dudley
(d. 1554)

[1]
Henry Herbert,
Earl of Pembroke
(d. 1601)
(marriage
dissolved)

m. Catherine
Grey
(d. 1568)

[2]
m. Edward
Seymour,
Earl of
Hertford
(d. 1621)

Mary
Grey
(d. 1578)

m. Thomas
Keyes
(d. 1571)

Select bibliography

Most of the contemporary diplomatic correspondence and other documents relating to Mary I and her times have been published verbatim, or in very full summaries, in

Letters and Papers of Henry VIII (London, 1862–1910)

Calendar of Spanish State Papers (London, 1862–1954)

Calendar of Venetian State Papers (London, 1864–1947)

Calendar of State Papers (Foreign Series) in the Reign of Edward VI (London, 1861)

Calendar of State Papers (Foreign Series) in the Reign of Mary (London, 1861)

Acts of the Privy Council (London, 1890–1907)

Ambassades de Noailles (in the original French) (Leyden, 1763)

A great deal of biassed but interesting information is found in

John Foxe, *Acts and Monuments* (The *Book of Martyrs*, first published in 1563 and 1570, best modern edition 1877), on the Protestant side; and

Henry Clifford, *Life of Jane Dormer, Duchess of Feria* (written in 1643, published London, 1887) on the Roman Catholic side.

Another contemporary source is the brief but invaluable entries in various diaries kept by courtiers and citizens of London during Mary's lifetime. These have been published under the titles

Wriothesley's Chronicle (London, 1875–7)

Chronicle of Queen Jane and Queen Mary (London, 1850)

Greyfriars Chronicle (London, 1852)

Machyn's Diary (London, 1848)

Spanish Chronicle (London, 1889).

The fullest modern biography of Mary I is

H.F.Prescott, *Mary Tudor* (London, 1953, revised edition, first published under the title *Spanish Tudor* in 1940).

Other biographies are

Beatrice White, *Mary Tudor* (London, 1935)

J.M.Stone, *The History of Mary I, Queen of England* (London, 1901)

The best account of the religious persecutions in Mary's lifetime is found in

R.W.Dixon, *History of the Church of England* (London, 1878–1902) from the Protestant viewpoint;

Philip Hughes, *The Reformation in England* (London, 1953), from the Roman Catholic viewpoint;

J.Gairdner, *Lollardy and the Reformation in England* (London, 1908–13), for the period up to 1554 (anti-Protestant).

Other books containing much useful information and comment about Mary are

G.Mattingly, *Catherine of Aragon* (London, 1942)

R.Tyler, *The Emperor Charles the Fifth* (London, 1956)

W.K.Jordan's two-volume book on Edward VI's reign, *Edward VI: The Young King* (London, 1968), and *Edward VI: The Threshold of Power* (London, 1970).

Index

223

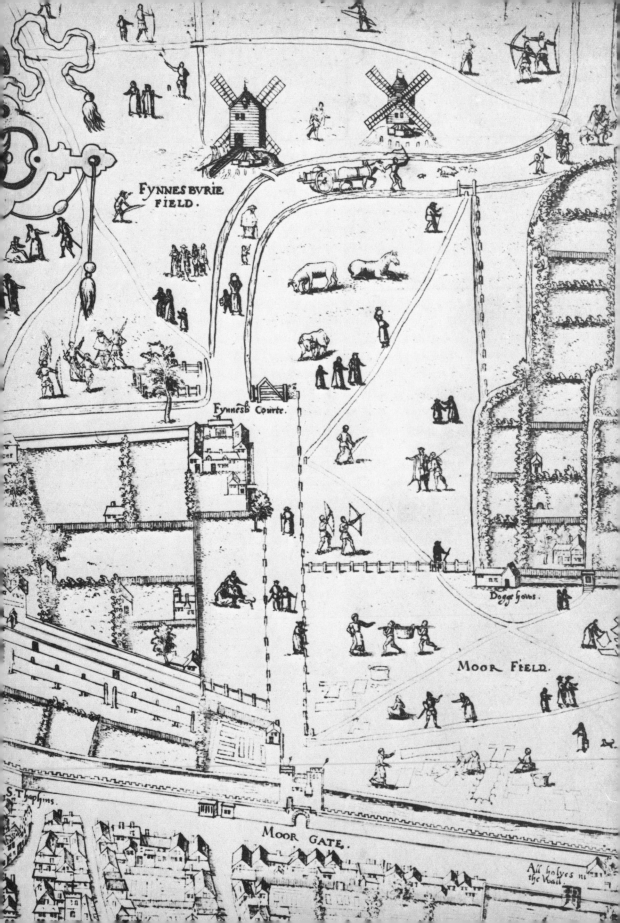

FYNNES BVRIE FIELD.

Fynnesb Courte.

Dogg hows.

MOOR FIELD.

S.T haphins.

MOOR GATE.

All holyes ni the Wall.